ASPECTS OF THE EPIC

The book is a collection of essays on various aspects of the epic tradition ranging from Homer to modern Greece. **Penelope Murray** considers the portrayal of the bard in Homeric epic laying particular emphasis on the relation of Homer's own biography to the fictional bards presented in the poems, and gives a new twist to the Homeric question. **G. S. Kirk** discusses the central problem of tradition and originality in oral poetry – is it possible to detect the mind of Homer himself amidst the vast mass of inherited material with which he works? – and argues by detailed examination of the text that books 5 and 6 of the *Iliad* are the product of Homer's unique genius. **John Gould** examines the seminal influence of Homer on the Greek tragedians and shows that, in spite of the obvious similarities between the two genres, Greek tragedy springs from a very different world from that of Homeric epic. **K. W. Gransden's** essay centres on the second half of the *Aeneid*, Virgil's *Iliad*, and illustrates the particularly Virgilian qualities of these books by comparison and contrast with their Homeric models. **John Bayley** looks at one aspect of the epic tradition, the theme of love, using examples from a wide range of epic material including Homer, Milton and Tolstoy. **Tom Winnifrith** explores the somewhat neglected subject of epic poetry in the Byzantine period, focusing his discussion on the epic of *Digenis Akritas*, and **Paul Merchant** extends the scope of the book to the present day with a consideration of the epic strain in modern Greek literature.

This book should appeal to anyone interested in the epic tradition in European literature.

ASPECTS OF
THE EPIC

Edited by
Tom Winnifrith,
Penelope Murray
and
K. W. Gransden

First published 1983 by
THE MACMILLAN PRESS LTD
London and Basingstoke
Companies and representatives
throughout the world

ISBN 0 333 30706 2

Printed in Hong Kong

883.009
A 838
c. 1

Contents

Acknowledgements

The editors would like to thank the Greek Embassy in London for sponsoring these lectures and for generous help in their preparation given by Mrs Christine Wyman and Mrs Janet Bailey. A special debt is owed to Mrs Eleni Cubitt.
Mr Gransden's essay is based on material for a book on Virgil's epic narrative to be published by the Cambridge University Press in 1983.

Notes on the Contributors

John Bayley is Warton Professor of English Literature at the University of Oxford. His books include *The Characters of Love* and *The Uses of Division: Unity and Disharmony in Literature*.

John Gould is Professor of Greek at the University of Bristol. He is the author of *The Development of Plato's Ethics* and has written on various aspects of Greek culture including Greek tragedy.

K.W. Gransden is Reader in English and Comparative Literary Studies at the University of Warwick. His works include *Virgil's Iliad* and editions of books VIII and XI of Virgil's *Aeneid*.

G.S. Kirk is Professor of Greek at the University of Cambridge. His books include *The Songs of Homer* and *Homer and the Oral Tradition*.

Paul Merchant is a Lecturer in English and Comparative Literary Studies at the University of Warwick. He is the author of *The Epic* and has published some of his poetry.

Penelope Murray is a Lecturer in Classical Literature at the University of Warwick and is co-editor of *Greece Old and New*.

Tom Winnifrith is a Senior Lecturer in English and Comparative Literary Studies at the University of Warwick. He has published works on the Brontës and is co-editor of *Greece Old and New*.

Preface

The six pieces in this book were originally delivered as a series of lectures organised by the School of Classical Civilisation at the University of Warwick in the autumn of 1980 and generously sponsored by the Greek Embassy. The contributors, who are mainly but not exclusively classical scholars, were invited to consider various aspects of the European epic tradition. Hence the variety of tone, range and treatment in the essays: if they have any unity, other than that which the reader will confer on them by the act of reading, it comes, as we should expect, from Homer. His name, or that of one of his poems, occurs in the title of all but one of the pieces, which move from a detailed study of two adjacent books of the *Iliad* to an account of the twentieth-century 'Homeridae' who flourish, largely unknown to English readers, in the land of Homer and who write in Greek - not Homer's Greek, but Greek none the less, a poetic continuity surely unparalleled elsewhere in Europe. Paul Merchant has included in his essay specimens of their work in his own translations: throughout this volume, no knowledge of Greek is necessarily assumed in the reader.

Homer did not only, for all practical purposes, invent the epic as a great literary form. He also, as Dr Murray says, invented the 'Homeric question'. Professor Kirk's contribution is a reminder of the complexity and persistence of that unanswerable conundrum even in an age which has relegated the old debate between analysts and unitarians to the history of scholarship and has realised that if we want to understand the *Iliad* and the *Odyssey* we must scrutinise them like any other literary texts, even though we know that they are not quite like any other literary texts. And in that paradox, perhaps the old 'question' pops up again. But as Professor Kirk says, the great poet is he who can go beyond the tradition and that is what Homer does. We may, if we will, see part of his own greatness in the greatness of the tradition he has gone beyond. His genius transformed - how

can we ever know how? – the 'songs on the lips of men' into
two monumental poems. No other genre has been so dominated
by its first exponent as the epic by Homer has. (One has
only to think of opera or the novel.) Even tragic drama
cannot owe so great a debt to Aeschylus as he himself owed
(and acknowledged) to Homer. In the *Agamemnon*, the Trojan
war has indeed become, as Professor Gould reminds us, sombre
and unheroic, yet there is a sense in which it was already
these things in the *Iliad*. Part of Homer's 'many-mindedness'
is that he includes his own antitheses. Reductive, anti-
heroic elements were already there, a Thersites against an
Achilles, and for all the talk of glory and the splendour of
flashing bronze 'the coward and the brave man, both have
died alike', and it was Achilles, not Thersites, who said
that. It is not just that the 'impersonal bard' comments on
his own tales, but the tales themselves contain moral
comment: the embassy to Achilles is only one of the more
obvious examples, as is the extraordinarily 'modern' treatment of Helen when we see her reflecting on her own
behaviour and what the world will make of it.

Since Homer, epic poetry has 'peaked' at certain great
moments in the later creative history of Europe. Eliot's
theory of 'Tradition and the Individual Talent' is particularly relevant to the genre:

> The existing monuments form an ideal order among
> themselves which is modified by the introduction of the
> new (the really new) work of art among them. The existing
> order is complete before the new work arrives; for order
> to persist after the supervention of novelty, the *whole*
> existing order must be, if ever so slightly, altered; and
> so the relations, proportions, values of each work towards
> the whole are readjusted . . .

Such moments in the after-life of Homeric epic occurred in
the flowering of tragic drama in fifth-century Athens, and
again when Virgil wrote the *Aeneid*. Thereafter the influence
of the *Iliad* and the *Odyssey* became more diffuse, as they
receded into the mists of darkness and ignorance, partially
dispelled in the Medieval and Byzantine worlds. With the
Renaissance we arrive at the hey-day of secondary epic. Comparative literature, that most modish of contemporary disciplines, has its roots deep in the polymathy of the
Renaissance, when the greatest writers - and, as Professor
Bayley reminds us, painters too - rediscovered the epic and
developed the 'heroic theme of love'. And that theme, too,
was Homer's. In Eve's appeal in *Paradise Lost*, X, 'Forsake
me not thus, Adam', we may hear - and the Renaissance poet

would have expected us to hear - the faint but unmistakeable
echo of Andromache's appeal to Hector, 'Come now, stay with
me here by the tower' and - stronger and nearer - the cries
of Dido to Aeneas. But Milton's Adam had a freedom of choice
denied to Aeneas and perhaps also to Hector. And therein
lies the strength of epic: it can mutate and reshape traditional motifs in accordance with the changing moral structure of society. The epic tradition is nothing less than a
continual authoritative redefining of human destiny.

K.W. Gransden

1 Homer and the Bard

PENELOPE MURRAY

Fashions in Homeric scholarship come and go. The analysts
and the Yugoslavs have had their day: it is now the turn of
the unitarians. Modern scholarship, it is clear, is devoting
more and more attention to the unity of the *Iliad* and the
Odyssey, and to their sophistication as epics organised by a
single mind with a single purpose in view - and rightly so.
To many scholars the only quasi-biographical question that
remains a puzzle is whether we suppose one Homer or two,
each man of genius responsible for a separate and individual
poem of genius. But Homer (and I use the word in either the
singular or the dual), Homer too has his view of the poet.
And the problem is to reconcile this view with the prevail-
ing orthodoxy. One of the strengths of the analyst position
was that it could point to Homer's own description of the
bard in its defence: the *Iliad* and the *Odyssey* were composed
of separate lays, composed it may be by separate persons, or
at least for separate occasions, and sung in the way that
Homer describes, as entertainments at the banquets of the
nobility. For example, in *Odyssey*, 8, Odysseus praises the
bard Demodocus for the song he has just sung and asks him to
change to another theme - the wooden horse and its
fashioning:

> The bard felt the prompting of the god and began
> his utterance of the lay, *taking it up* where
> the Argives had set their huts aflame . . .
> > (*Odyssey*, 8. 499-501)[1]

I take another example from Book 1 of the *Odyssey* when
Penelope, saddened by Phemius' singing, comes down to the
hall where the suitors are enjoying the bard's music:

> With sudden tears she spoke to the heaven-taught bard:
> 'Phemius, you know many other lays to beguile men's
> hearts, deeds of heroes and deeds of gods that the bards

1

sing of; choose one of those and sing it among the suitors
here while they drink their wine in silence, but cease
from this melancholy lay that always wrings my
heart within me'.

(Odyssey, 1. 336-42)

Such descriptions suggest individual lays with individual
structures, suited, it may be, to particular audiences or at
least existing as separate entities. It is not easy to see
how poems of the length of the *Iliad* and *Odyssey* could find
their place in the banquets described by Homer unless these
banquets extended far beyond the rosy-fingered dawn. Nor is
it easy to see how the unity postulated by the most recent
scholarship on Homer could result from the combination of
such separate lays if that unity were to be the creation of
a poet trained in such a school of aristocratic entertainment. One of the most pressing problems therefore posed by
the modern tendency to regard the *Iliad* and the *Odyssey* as
unities is how this attitude can be reconciled with what
Homer himself says about the nature of the poet, the practice of poetry and the occasions of its performance. It was
easy to avoid all biographical questions when Homer was
thought to be a guild: a group cannot have a biography, it
merely has habits. But once we begin to believe that Homer
is one man (or two), it necessarily follows that he must *in
fact* have had a biography (or two biographies). To some this
may seem a trivial question, of interest only to those who
already believe in the biographical fallacy. But, as we
shall see, the question is not as simple or as trivial as it
may appear at first sight. In order to attempt to answer
these questions we must, of course, begin from what the
Homeric poems say about the position of the poet and the
function of his poetry, and then try to understand to what
extent these statements are compatible with the hypotheses
of modern scholarship.

In the *Odyssey* the bard is characteristically seen singing
for the entertainment of nobles at banquets. When Telemachus
arrives at the palace of Menelaus at the opening of Book 4
he finds

guests feasting in the great lofty hall, neighbours
and clansmen of glorious Menelaus; they were making
merry, and in their midst an inspired bard (θεῖος ἀοιδός)
was singing to the lyre, while a pair of tumblers along
the line of guests twisted and twirled to the rhythms of
the singer.

(Odyssey, 4. 15-19)

On Ithaca the bard Phemius sings for the pleasure of the
suitors as they feast in Odysseus' palace; and in Phaeacia
Demodocus is constantly being summoned to crown the
pleasures of the banquet with his music. As Odysseus says:

> truly it is a happy thing to listen to such a bard
> as this, whose utterance is like a god's. Indeed I think
> life is at its best when a whole people is in festivity
> and banqueters in the hall sit next to each other listen-
> ing to the bard, while the tables by them are laden with
> bread and meat, and the cupbearer draws wine from the
> mixing-bowl and pours it into the cups.
>
> (*Odyssey*, 9. 3-10)

Clearly, then, one of the chief functions, if not *the* chief
function, of the bard in Homeric society is to give pleasure;
and the frequency of the word τέρπειν (to delight) in
connexion with music generally in both epics underlines the
importance of this aspect of song. In the *Iliad* (Book 9)
even Achilles finds pleasure in singing κλέα ἀνδρῶν (the
glorious deeds of men) to the accompaniment of a lyre. And
on the divine level the gods enjoy the music of the Muses
and Apollo at their feasts, as at the end of *Iliad*, Book 1.
    The celebration of κλέα ἀνδρῶν is another very important
function of poetry which Homer is careful to emphasise. The
glorious deeds of men are the subject of almost all the lays
sung by bards within the poems, and indeed of the *Iliad* and
the *Odyssey* themselves. Through his characters Homer makes
us well aware of the poet's ability to confer everlasting
fame on contemporary events. At the end of *Odyssey*, 8, for
example, Alcinous says that the sufferings of Greeks and
Trojans at Troy were devised by the gods so that they could
be the subject of song for future generations. Agamemnon's
ghost in Hades envies Odysseus his faithful Penelope:

> the fame of her virtue will never die, and the Deathless
> Ones will see to it that men on earth have a lovely song
> in honour of chaste Penelope. Not so will it be with the
> daughter of Tyndareos. She plotted evil, she slew her
> wedded husband, and the song of her among mankind will be
> one of loathing.
>
> (*Odyssey*, 24. 196-201)

In the *Iliad* (6.357-8) Helen knows that she and Paris will
be the subject of song for future generations: she sees herself as the theme of poetry. It is interesting that in all
these examples the events which the characters describe as
suitable subjects for poetry are in fact the events of the

Iliad and *Odyssey* : the fate of the Achaeans at Troy, and
Helen's part in that fate; the return of Odysseus, the
faithfulness of Penelope, and so on. In other words it is
impossible for the reader or listener *not* to see a reference
to Homer's own poetry here. Homer knows that his song will
be immortal, and makes sure that his audience knows this
too.

A third aspect of poetry which Homeric epic stresses is
its affective power. Penelope (*Odyssey*, 1.337) describes the
bard's songs as θελκτήρια (charms or spells), a word which
perhaps still retains some of its magical associations - at
any rate the related verb θέλγειν (to enchant or bewitch) is
used of the truly magical power of the siren's song in
Odyssey, 12 as well as of the bard's effect on his listen-
ers. We are given a vivid glimpse of the enthralled attention of the audience in *Odyssey*, 17 when Eumaeus describes
the disguised Odysseus' effect on him:

> It was just as when one keeps gazing at a bard whom the
> gods have taught to give joy to mortals with his song, and
> whenever he begins to sing, men gladly would listen to him
> for ever - so did this man enchant my ears as he sat
> beside me.
>
> (*Odyssey*, 17. 518-21)

I note here the interesting fact that Odysseus himself is on
several occasions compared to a bard: he enchants Eumaeus
like a bard in the passage just quoted, earlier on (*Odyssey*,
11.368) Alcinous praises Odysseus for putting together his
tale skilfully like a bard, and at the climactic point of
the poem when Odysseus strings the bow he is again compared
with a bard:

> like a master of lyre and song who with utmost ease winds
> a new string round a peg, fitting the pliant sheepgut at
> either end, so did Odysseus string the great bow tran-
> quilly.
>
> (*Odyssey*, 21. 406-9)

Could it be that Homer is deliberately glorifying himself
and his own profession by associating his hero so closely
with the bard?

Apart from the magical power of poetry, we are also shown
specific emotional reactions to song. Penelope weeps when
she hears Phemius singing of the sorrowful homecoming of the
Achaeans from Troy (*Odyssey*, 1.336); even the brave and much
enduring Odysseus is reduced to tears by the bard's singing:

These were the things the great bard sang of. Odysseus
meanwhile was greatly moved, and down from his eyes the
tears came coursing over his cheeks. It was as when a
woman weeps with her arms around her darling husband, one
who has been defending his country and countrymen,
striving to keep the day of mercilessness far from his
city and his children, but now has fallen and is dying and
gasping out his life. She gazes at him, she clings to him
and she shrieks aloud, but the victors behind her, with
their spears, beat her on back and shoulders and lead her
away into captivity to suffer lamentable oppression; her
cheeks are wasted with piteous sorrow. So from Odysseus'
eyes the tears fell piteously.

(*Odyssey*, 8. 521-31)

That emotive and typically Homeric simile graphically
depicts the strength of Odysseus' reaction to Demodocus'
song. It is interesting that this emphasis on the powerful
emotional effect of poetry remained central to the Greek
conception of poetry throughout antiquity: it played a major
part in Plato's attack on poetry, and in Aristotle's defence
of it; it also formed the basis of Longinus' theory of the
sublime. But that is another subject.

So far I have discussed the three aspects which seem to be
most prominent in Homer's conception of poetry: poetry has
the duty and the power to give pleasure, to celebrate κλέα
ἀνδρῶν and to move its audience. I turn now to the view of
the *bard* presented in the Homeric poems.

The epithet most commonly used to describe the bard is
θεῖος (divine). This epithet is conventional and has
undoubtedly lost much of its original force in Homer - no
one imagines that Phemius and Demodocus are literally divine
- nor is it used exclusively of bards; it is also used of
heralds and of certain individual heroes. Nevertheless the
epithet is significant, for the man who is θεῖος, be he
herald, hero or bard, is especially favoured by the gods.
The other epithets used of bards are περικλυτός (famous,
renowned), ἐρίηρος (faithful, trusty), ἥρως (hero) and
λαοῖσι τετιμένος (honoured by the people). An examination of
these epithets is revealing: we find that the epithet
ἐρίηρος is normally used with the word ἑταῖρος (comrade,
companion) to denote a comrade of lower rank than the person
whose comrade he is. Thus, for example, Odysseus' companions
who are to return to Ithaca with him are called ἐρίηρες
ἑταῖροι. Similarly the word ἥρως, besides denoting royal
persons, is also used of various θεράποντες (squires or
attendants). These epithets seem to suggest that the bard is
closely connected with the aristocracy, but subordinate to

it. The epithet περικλυτός also points to the same conclusion: in the *Odyssey* Hephaestus is the only other living
being who is called περικλυτός; he, like the bard, is famous
and respected because of his art, but is not the equal of
the Olympian gods whom he serves. But the Homeric bard is
not only connected with the aristocracy: the very name
Demodocus (which means something like 'esteemed by the
people') and the epithet λαοῖσι τετιμένος suggest an association with the people. And at *Odyssey*, 17.383 the bard is
classed as a δημιοεργός (a public worker) together with the
seer, the healer of diseases, and the carpenter. That in
fact constitutes a list of the professional men of the
Heroic Age: each of them is the master of some craft which
can be of service to the community at large. Thus although
the Homeric bard is primarily depicted as a court poet,
singing for the entertainment of the aristocracy, we should
not neglect his association with the people.

In general the bard is described sympathetically and in
terms of respect, even though he is not always treated res-
pectfully by the characters within the poems. Demodocus is
all right: he is always politely escorted by a herald, and
given as much food and wine as he wants. Odysseus pays him a
particular compliment when he cuts off a portion, rich in
fat, from the chine of a white tusked boar, and bids the
herald give it to the bard:

> Here, young man; let Demodocus have this dish to eat; I
> must do him this courtesy, sad though my mood is. For in
> all men's eyes all over the world bards deserve honour and
> veneration, because the goddess of song has taught them
> lays and has shown her favour to all their brotherhood.
>
> (*Odyssey*, 8. 477-81)

Phemius, however, is less fortunate: he is forced to sing
for the suitors against his will (ἀνάγκη), as we are told on
more than one occasion. We do not see him being maltreated,
but it is evident that he chooses themes which will be particularly pleasing to his audience of suitors. When Penelope
in *Odyssey*, 1 asks Phemius to stop singing of the sorrowful
homecoming of the Achaeans from Troy Telemachus rebukes her
on the grounds that the bard has the right to please his
audience by any path that his fancy takes; besides 'men will
applaud most eagerly whatever song falls freshest upon the
listening ear'. What he does *not* add is that a song which
reminds the suitors of Odysseus' misfortunes is certainly
going to please them. In this case Phemius' fancy has taken
him along a path which leads straight to his audience's
heart. A bard who *is* maltreated is the anonymous bard whom

Agamemnon left behind to guard Clytaemnestra when he went to
Troy (*Odyssey*, 3.267-71). At first Clytaemnestra resisted
Aegisthus' attempts to seduce her because the bard was there
to protect her: 'But when the gods' purpose ordained that
she should yield, Aegisthus carried the bard away to a
desert island and left him there to become the spoil of
birds of prey.' In this episode Homer goes out of his way to
emphasise the virtuous part played by the bard - why does
the bard appear at all if not to draw attention to the
importance of Homer's own profession? - and Aegisthus' shameful treatment of him serves to underline the latter's own
wickedness.

The bard *ought* to be revered not least because he has a
special relationship with the divine, as Odysseus explicitly
says in the passage I have already quoted. This link with
the divine is expressed in a number of different ways: we
are told that the Muses love bards, teach them and give them
the gift of poetry. Homer does not tell us precisely what
the gift of poetry entails, nor does he speculate as to the
reasons for its bestowal; but it is evidently a permanent
gift of poetic ability. See, for example, Alcinous' words:

> Summon . . . the sacred bard Demodocus, because on him
> more than on any other the god has bestowed the gift of
> song, to delight men on whatever theme he may be
> inspirited to sing.
>
> (*Odyssey*, 8. 43-5)

It is, of course, important to remember that poetry is not
the only activity which Homer regards as divine - an obvious
point, but one which is often overlooked. Examples of particular attributes and skills which Homer describes as
divine gifts (apart from poetry) are physical beauty, handi-
work, strength, might and wisdom, eloquence and prophecy.
What is significant is that the gift idiom, like the
teaching idiom, is used primarily to describe outstanding
abilities or distinguishing features. The bard's poetic
ability is conceived of as a gift of divinity because, like
other outstanding abilities, it is not explicable in purely
human terms. This general point was noted by Castelvetro in
his annotation of Aristotle's *Poetics* (1571):

> Anything done by someone else is highly regarded and seems
> marvellous to those who have not the power to do it them-
> selves, and because men commonly measure the forces of the
> body and of the ability of other men by comparison with
> their own, they reckon as a miracle and a special gift of
> God that which they do not know how to attain by their own

natural powers, and see that others have attained.

The Homeric notion of poetry as a gift of the gods is in
fact the equivalent of subsequent notions of poetic genius.
  I have claimed that the divine gift of poetry is a permanent one; but the case of Thamyris in *Iliad*, 2 shows that it
is not always so. Once in Dorium, we are told

> The Muses met Thamyris the Thracian and stopped his
> singing. . . . For he boasted that he would beat the Muses,
> the daughters of Zeus the aegis-bearer, if they were to
> sing against him. But they were angry and maimed him, and
> took away from him his wonderful singing and made him
> forget his musical ability.
>
> (*Iliad*, 2. 594-600)

Homer does not specify the particular disability which the
Muses inflicted on Thamyris, but we learn from other sources
that they blinded him. Clearly they did so, and removed from
him his gift of song, as a punishment for misusing the gift
which he had been given. Scholars point out that this story
is particularly intelligible if, as is often claimed, the
Muses were originally mountain nymphs, since encounters with
nymphs have always been considered dangerous. But in any
case the Muses' punishment of Thamyris is consistent with
the general picture which we have of the way in which the
Greek gods dealt with overweening mortals. This story, with
its characteristically Greek emphasis on the great divide
between gods and men, indicates that what the Muses can give,
they can also take away. The most accurate formulation, then,
of the gift idiom and others like it is that the Muses
bestow on bards an ability which is normally permanent, but
which they can take away if they consider it has been
misused.
  In Thamyris' case, blindness was inflicted on him by the
Muses as a punishment, and at the same time he lost his gift
of song. By contrast Demodocus was blinded, but received the
gift of song in compensation:

> The Muse had favoured him above others, yet had given him
> good and evil mingled; his eyes she took from him, but she
> gave him entrancing song.
>
> (*Odyssey*, 8. 63-4)

This idea, which perhaps foreshadows subsequent theories of
the compensatory nature of art, is found elsewhere in Greek
literature. Homer himself was said to have been blind - a
legend which was no doubt derived at least in part from the

picture of Demodocus in the *Odyssey* - the other obvious
source for this legend is the *Homeric Hymn to Apollo* in
which the poet asks to be remembered as 'the blind man of
Chios'. At any rate the author of an anonymous *Life of Homer*
clearly regards Homer's poetic ability as compensatory, in
his somewhat fanciful account of the circumstances surrounding the poet's blinding:

> This is how he was blinded, they say: he went to Achilles'
> tomb and begged to see the hero just as he was when he
> went into battle dressed in the second suit of armour.
> But on seeing Achilles, Homer was blinded by the bright-
> ness of his armour. Thetis and the Muses pitied him and he
> was honoured with the art of poetry.
>
> (*Vita*, VI. 45-51, ed. T.W. Allen)

The gift of prophecy too was evidently regarded as compensatory, as we learn from several accounts of Teiresias'
blinding. According to one version of the story (Hesiod,
275) Zeus made Teiresias a prophet after he had been blinded
by Hera; according to another (Callimachus, *Hymn*, 5. 75-130)
Athena blinded him because he had seen her bathing, but she
subsequently gave him the gift of prophecy in compensation.
Herodotus (9.93) tells the tale of a certain Evenius, who
was blinded by the people of Apollonia for failing to guard
their sacred sheep, and subsequently given the gift of prophecy by the gods. In these stories about Homer, Teiresias
and Evenius, the compensatory nature of their gifts is made
explicit.

In Demodocus' case there is a second implication: that is
that the gift of poetry is so special that it must be paid
for in some way. Again there is a parallel for this in the
realm of prophecy: Phineus, according to Hesiod (*fr.* 157),
was asked by the gods whether he would prefer to be a seer
and be maimed or to live for a short time and in good
health, but without the gift of prophecy. He chose to be a
seer, whereupon Apollo blinded him. In other words the gift
of prophecy is here regarded as inseparable from blindness.
Although the point is not made explicitly in Demodocus'
case, it is surely implied. The gift of poetic ability is
seen as both a compensation for blindness and the cause of
it.

This frequent association of blindness with poets and
prophets deserves comment. In the first place, these tales
may well reflect a true situation: it would be natural for
the blind to become bards in Homeric society, since they
would be unable to take part in many other occupations.
Blind people have good memories, and in an oral culture

memory is, of course, a vital factor in poetry. But whilst
there is no reason to doubt that the blind poet was a familiar figure in Ancient Greece, I would not be prepared to
vouch for the truth of any one of the stories that I have
considered.

As well as perhaps reflecting a true situation, the association of blindness with poetry and prophecy undoubtedly
has a symbolic significance which the Greeks recognised. For
the stories about blind poets and prophets imply that these
people have a special kind of sight: they lose their physical
sight, but they gain something better - inner sight or
vision. In early Greek literature there is a very close connexion between knowledge and sight, indeed the connexion is
inherent in the Greek language: οἶδα (I know) is from the
same verb as ἰδεῖν (to see). In the *Iliad* when the poet asks
the Muses for inspiration in the long and detailed invocation before the catalogue of ships (Book 2) he specifically
says that the Muses know everything because they, as
goddesses, have seen everything. In the *Odyssey* (Book 8)
Odysseus is amazed at the bard's knowledge of what happened
to the Achaeans - it was as if he had actually been there.
It is particularly interesting that Odysseus should say this
to Demodocus, who was, after all, blind.

In fact it is clear that for Homer and the early Greek
poets in general the gift of poetry is closely bound up with
knowledge. It is no accident that the invocations in the
Iliad and *Odyssey* are essentially requests for information,
which the Muses, as daughters of Memory, provide. Through
the Muses the poet has access to knowledge which is denied
to ordinary mortals. And in this respect the gift of poetry
is similar to the gift of prophecy: both involve the acqui-
sition of divine knowledge.

If we bear in mind the intimate connexion between knowledge and sight in early Greek literature, the significance
of the stories about blind poets and prophets becomes clear.
These stories contrast the special, divine sight, that is,
knowledge of the poet (or prophet) with the ordinary sight
of man. Demodocus, for example, is deprived of human sight,
but is given something better: divine sight, or knowledge.
The implications of superior sight contained in the symbol
of the blind *prophet* are made clear in Sophocles' *Oedipus
Tyrannus*: a central theme of that play is the contrast
between the sight of the blind Teiresias and the blindness
of the sighted Oedipus. The contrary idea that the majority
of mortals are (metaphorically) blind occurs frequently in
early Greek literature. Pindar, for example, (*Paean*, 7b. 15-
20) prays to Mnemosyne and her daughters to give him skill
in invention 'for men's minds are blind, if anyone seeks out

the steep path of wisdom without the Heliconian Muses'. If
men's minds are blind without the Muses, the obvious implication is that, with the help of the Muses, men can see: the
poet is the man to whom the Muses grant the power of vision,
and his physical blindness serves to remind us of this. It
is also the price he has to pay for the gift of divine sight
or knowledge. There is an interesting parallel for this idea
in Celtic legend in which a drink from a spring containing
information and wisdom has to be paid for by the loss of an
eye.[2]

*   *   *

The Homeric bard is an inspired being, blessed with the gift
of divine knowledge; but he is also a craftsman, responsible
for his own creations. I have already referred to the
passage in the *Odyssey* in which the bard is described as a
δημιοεργός, a public worker who is the master of a craft.
For Homer there is no contradiction between these two views
of the poet. The two aspects of craftsmanship and inspiration come together most memorably in Phemius' words to
Odysseus when he is begging for his life:

> In supplication I come to you, Odysseus; hold me in rever-
> ence, have compassion. You yourself will repent it after-
> wards if you kill a man like me, a bard, singing for gods
> and men alike. I am self-taught; the god has implanted in
> my breast all manner of ways of song.
>
> (*Odyssey*, 22. 344-8)

These words are not easy to understand, and many different
interpretations of them have been offered. But I think one
point is clear: the two halves of his statement are not
contradictory if we consider them in the context of Homer's
language as a whole: it is quite normal in Homeric epic for
actions to be described in both human and divine terms, and
in general a god's prompting does not exclude a personal
motivation. There is nothing contradictory, therefore, in
Phemius' claim that he is both self-taught and the recipient
of divine aid. But what does he mean? The word αὐτοδίδακτος
(self taught) clearly implies a notion of skill or technique,
as well as a pride in his own particular way of singing; but
he cannot mean that he is literally self-taught: no bard,
however inspired, could discover for himself all the tech-
niques of oral poetry. Perhaps what he means is that he does
not simply repeat songs he has learnt from other bards, but
composes his songs himself. In other words, what he is
claiming for himself is originality in the context of oral

poetry. This interpretation is supported by the words of a
Kara-Kirghiz bard, which are surprisingly close to Phemius'
claim:

> I can sing every song; for God has planted the gift of
> song in my heart. He gives me the word on my tongue
> without my having to seek it. I have learned none of my
> songs. All springs up from my inner being and goes forth
> from it.[3]

*   *   *

No-one in antiquity knew who Homer was. His date was variously given as contemporary with the Trojan War, soon after
it, at the time of the Ionian migration, the mid-ninth century or 500 years after the Trojan War. His place of birth
was a matter of dispute: Chios, Smyrna, Colophon, Athens,
Cyprus and Egypt were amongst the contenders. His parentage
was the subject of wild fantasies: his father was the god
Apollo, a δαίμων, a river; his mother was a nymph or the
Muse Calliope. Alternatively he was born of quite ordinary
parents, but was nursed by a prophetess from whose breasts
honey poured into the mouth of the infant Homer. Elaborate
genealogies were constructed relating him to legendary poets
such as Linus, Musaeus and Orpheus. He was traditionally
said to have been blind, and his name was falsely etymolo-
gised as ὁ μὴ ὁρῶν - he who sees not. Various stories were
made up about the circumstances surrounding his blindness:
according to one of the more colourful versions Helen
blinded him because she was angry with him for spreading
rumours about her elopement with Paris.

The biographical tradition about Homer clearly reflects a
complete ignorance of his true biography. Like most other
ancient biographies it is made up of two different elements.
It is a commonplace of modern scholarship that ancient
biographers derived information about the lives of their
subjects from their works. So, for example, Anacreon, the
poet of wine, was said to have choked to death on a grape
pip. Alcaeus, it was claimed, wrote his poetry while drunk,
and indeed was found to be drinking at all times and in all
circumstances. Philetas, exponent of the slender style, was
said to have been so thin himself that he had to wear lead
soles on his shoes so as not to be blown away by the wind.
The Homeric poems provide little material of this type for
the biographer of Homer. On the other hand it was, and perhaps is, a reasonable supposition to regard Homer as one of
the bards he describes. Demodocus is obviously the favourite.

So, in the earliest biographical evidence of all, the sixth
century *Homeric Hymn to Apollo*, we find the bard saying:

> Remember me in the future, whenever anyone of men who
> inhabit the earth, a stranger who has endured much, comes
> here and asks: "Girls, who is the sweetest bard who comes
> here, and who gives you the greatest pleasure?" Then you
> must all with one accord answer, saying of me: "A blind
> man, who lives in rocky Chios (τυφλὸς ἀνήρ, οἰκεῖ δὲ Χίῳ
> ἔνι παιπαλοέσσῃ); his songs are all supreme for the time
> to come."

In antiquity this was universally taken to be an autobio-
graphical description by Homer, though we now regard it as
the claim of a later poet that he was Homer. The motif of
blindness is already present here and is surely based on the
picture of Demodocus in the *Odyssey*. But no one seems to have
asked the question whether Homer intended the blindness of
his bard to be metaphorical or literal. We cannot know
whether the most basic and widely believed fact about
Homer's biography - that he was blind - is true.

A second thread in the biographical tradition is the free
invention of stories thought typical or appropriate to the
poet. For example, nightingales sang on the lips of the
infant Stesichorus; bees smeared honey on Pindar's lips when
he was a child; before his birth, Apollo foretold that
Archilochus would be immortal, and so on. All such anecdotes
merely reflect the attitude of a later generation to poets
in general or to the particular poet in question. They stand
in the same relation to truth as Samuel Butler's claim that
Homer was a woman.

It is easy enough to criticise the ancient practice of
extracting information about the lives of poets from their
poetry. But how different is that from the modern practice,
exemplified by myself in this paper, of assuming that
Homer's view of himself and his craft can be derived from
the view of poets and poetry presented in the Homeric poems?
Does Homer really mean us to take the pictures of Phemius
and Demodocus and the statements about the function of
poetry within his epics as a sort of poetic biography of
himself?

In one sense it is clear that he does: indeed he deliberately invites us to do so. First of all he draws attention
to the bard in contexts where we would not normally expect
to find him. For example, as I have already said, Odysseus
himself is on several occasions compared with a bard. Agamemnon, before departing for Troy, entrusts Clytaemnestra to
a bard. Why should it be a *bard* who is singled out to

protect her? Again, why does Homer introduce the story of
the poet Thamyris into the catalogue of ships in the *Iliad*?
Secondly Homer makes sure that the subjects of the *Iliad* and
the *Odyssey* are seen as the ordinary theme of the Homeric
bards. It is not just the Trojan War or the generation of
epic heroes that stands at the centre of the Homeric bard's
interest: it is precisely the *Iliad* and the *Odyssey*. As I
pointed out earlier the events which the characters in the
poems describe as suitable subjects for poetry are in fact
the events of the *Iliad* and *Odyssey*: the fate of the
Achaeans at Troy, and Helen's part in that fate; the return
of Odysseus, the faithfulness of Penelope. In *Odyssey*, 8 we
find Demodocus choosing to sing a lay, whose theme is a
quarrel - not the quarrel between Agamemnon and Achilles,
but nevertheless a *quarrel*:

> He chose the lay whose fame had reached to broad heaven
> itself, the quarrel between Odysseus and Achilles . . .
>   (*Odyssey*, 8. 74-5)

And in Book 1 of the *Odyssey* we see the bard Phemius singing
of the *return* of the Achaeans from Troy. This seems to be a
deliberate attempt on Homer's part to identify himself with
his own portrayal of the Homeric bard; he invites us to see
himself as part of his own imaginary world.

   Most of my examples have been taken from the *Odyssey*, and
it might, I suppose, be held that there is a difference
between the view of poets and poetry presented in the two
epics. If such a view could be upheld, it would be strong
evidence for the existence of two Homers. But I do not
believe that any such difference can be detected. The greater interest in poets and poetry in the *Odyssey* represents
the self-absorption and concern for his art characteristic
of the older man. The *Odyssey* is Homer's *Tempest*.

   But there are obvious historical reasons why this 'poetic
autobiography' cannot be wholly true: the poetry of Homer's
bards consists of a succession of different lays, yet
Homer's poems are too long, and, as modern scholarship has
emphasised, too unified to be sung as separate lays. Phemius
and Demodocus are essentially court poets singing about
recent events, but Homer himself was not composing poems on
the exploits of the contemporary lords of rocky Chios: the
only epic about the colonisation of the West was the *Odyssey*;
the only epic about the Lelantine War was the *Iliad*. And
there are other indications that the picture Homer draws of
himself is not true to life. Many modern scholars, for
example, would believe that the Homeric text as we have it
owes something in some way to the invention of writing in

Greece. It is not so much that Homer is unaware of the existence of writing - the story of Bellerophon (*Iliad*, 6) shows clearly that he was well aware of its existence - but he is also well aware that writing cannot appear in a heroic context.

There is, therefore, an essential ambiguity here. What does it consist in and what is the explanation of it? I suggest that these problems, both ancient and modern, are the consequence of a deliberate paradox created by Homer. He wants us to believe that he is just one of a traditional group of ἀοιδοί, singers of lays; he sets himself in a tradition which goes back to the Bronze Age. But he knows perfectly well that he is no such thing. Homer has deliberately obscured his biography: it was Homer himself who invented the Homeric question.

NOTES

1. I quote here, and throughout this paper, from the recent translation of the *Odyssey* by W. Shewring (Oxford, 1980).
2. H.M. and N.K. Chadwick, *The Growth of Literature*, vol.I (Cambridge, 1932) pp.648-9.
3. Ibid., vol.III, p.182.

2 The *Iliad*: the Style of Books 5 and 6

G. S. KIRK

The question whether the *Iliad* is a unity has developed over
the years into a less crude one in its implications than
that debated by analysts and unitarians of the nineteenth
and early twentieth century. Even now, however, the question
tends to be put in ambiguous terms that lead to much scholarly confusion and misunderstanding.

It is now broadly recognised that tradition played a large
part in the constitution of the *Iliad*, as also did the particular artistry and creativity of one man, the ultimate
shaper and composer of the monumental poem, who was called
Homer. By 'tradition' we mean traditional heroic poetry,
sung over several generations by earlier singers, on which
Homer drew in many different ways. Thus in a sense the *Iliad*
does have different 'layers' of composition here and there,
according to Homer's use of older and younger inherited
material on the one hand and his own special adaptations and
innovations on the other. Different layers and a single composer used to be held to be contradictory, one had to choose
between them; but now, with fuller understanding of the
nature of oral poetry and the methods of its practitioners
in modern times, they can be seen as complementary in many
cases. And yet the arguments continue: Homer may have used
traditional materials, but was he himself a traditional
singer? Must he not have used writing to compose an epic so
large and so intricate? Could he have improvised poetry of
the subtlety and self-consistency of most of the *Iliad*? Most
such questions pick over, yet once again, the old problem of
authorship without revealing much that is new about the
nature of the epic itself. The terminology employed even by
generally sophisticated exponents of oral poetry (like A.B.
Lord and Ruth Finnegan)[1] is dangerously imprecise; the verb
'improvise' alone has created a hundred misunderstandings -
for example, it is often maintained that the *Iliad* cannot be

an oral poem because no oral poet could have *improvised* a
poem of that length! But the truth is that oral poets almost
never improvise, in the sense of pouring forth something
basically new and never thought about before. They may
occasionally do so in the manner of the least interesting
kind of musical improvising, in which familiar phrases and
formulas are juggled around in fresh combinations; but
actually *their* technique is more concerned with carefully
assimilating a large store of verses, passages and motifs
that with practice and ingenuity can be adapted to a variety
of different characters and plots. That is something the
guslari in Yugoslavia can be seen doing, not very well for
the most part, when they attempt to construct a piece that
is more personal and more ambitious than those of their
usual repertoire. Normally, however, they listen to other
singers, practice hard, and gradually over the years build
up a repertory of songs that vary slightly from performance
to performance because the singers occasionally omit a theme
or transfer a detail from one song to another. Homer, like
these people but at a far higher level, was a professional;
he practised hard, he assimilated not only formulaic phrases
and verses but also motifs and themes, which he aggregated
into whole songs of varying length not by improvisation, not
extempore, but by hard work, deliberate choice and developed
instinct. At this point the question about writing is of
little interest; it is certain that neither the availability
of writing materials, nor the novelty of the alphabet in
Greece, nor the effect of writing on his control of the oral
technique, would have made it easy for him to write out an
Iliad of anything like the kind that survives. Other possibilities (of writing down lists of episodes and the like or
of dictating parts, at least, to a scribe) cannot be entirely dismissed but again do not seem either especially attractive or especially significant.

What is more important in this whole matter of composition
is to see if we can how Homer, the monumental composer, uses
his tradition, and how much the brilliant success of the
epic as a whole is caused by the interaction between his
materials and his own creativity - between the general mass
of available heroic poetry (much of it probably of quite
high quality) and the particular skills and intentions he
applies to it in selecting from it, adapting it, using it
for the elaboration of his own most personal and creative
poetry in the traditional mould. For the most part that kind
of distinction of the 'specially Homeric' probably lies
beyond us, and the amalgam of traditional poetry and individual contribution remains impenetrable. Much of the battle-
action, for instance, is clearly drawn from the tradition.

We may strongly suspect that here and there, say in the
adducing of pathetic contextual details for a victim, Homer
is especially at work, but we cannot be really sure; for
much of that kind of detailed comment is common enough to be
regarded as typical, as an element, that is, of the tradition. Homer may have drawn on it more often than other
singers, he may have composed (always out of traditional
formulaic materials) some especially brilliant passages of
this kind, but we cannot be sure - and we cannot use much of
the battle-poetry by itself, without other and special
criteria, as a means of identifying his own individual style
as a singer, an *aoidos*.

I tried some years ago, in a lecture called 'The search
for the real Homer',[2] to see what other criteria might be
used. There I suggested, first that episodes described on an
unusually large scale, that is, in a leisurely way and with
relatively little narrative content, were probably made for
a monumental poem and not for those shorter poems, of say
500 to 1000 verses, that are likely to have been the standard oral unit. That happens to point most clearly to Book
14 of the *Odyssey*, which one is perhaps reluctant to see as
especially or typically Homeric. A better criterion may be
intrinsic connexion not with the length but with the crucial
turning-points of the large-scale plot. That more promising-
ly distinguishes the scenes of Hector's death in *Iliad*, 22
and Patroclus' in 16, together with the death of Sarpedon at
Patroclus' hands which shortly precedes it. Here, in addi-
tion, one can point to the presence of untypical details,
like the speech delivered just before death, in each scene;
and the conclusion does seem to emerge that something is to
be found here of Homer's special conception and individual
style in action. He is going beyond the tradition, developing it into something deeper and more abstract. Now I want
to look further, to find if there are other criteria that
might be applied in order to detect the master-poet at work
with broader and less severe materials. My criterion this
time will be even more obvious, in a way, than those tried
out before. It is, in short, the close connexion of a substantial, coherent but otherwise indeterminate episode or
sequence of episodes with another that can be recognised as
Homeric for independent reasons. Of course everything in the
Iliad has a certain common component of metre, formularity
and so on; obviously more than that will be required to
associate a particular passage with Homer himself, as we see
him at work in indispensable parts of the narrative core.
But let me begin from my unarguably Homeric constituent and
show the kind of association I have in mind. That manifestly
Homeric starting-point is Book 6 of the *Iliad* and in

particular the major section of it that describes Hector's
return to Troy and his encounters there. The associated
material will then (I believe) turn out to be the whole of
Book 5 and the latter part, at least, of 4: the triumph of
Diomedes, that means, which also extends into 6, and the
inspection of Agamemnon and opening of the fighting in 4.
But for simplicity's sake the argument will concentrate
mainly on 6 and 5.

To begin with, then, there is a certain unexpectedness in
this conjunction that makes it worth arguing about; the subjects and styles of the two books are so different, and that
in itself will tell us something important about Homer if
the case is made. It is not quite like maintaining, for
example, that Book 17 is Homeric because it arises solely
out of the main event of the 'core' Book 16, namely the
slaying of Patroclus. Book 17 explores in fine detail the
to-and-fro fighting for possession of his body; it is incon-
ceivable in a way that this should not be mostly by Homer,
given that 16 and the death of Patroclus substantially are
so. In this case, then, the argument from association leads
to an obvious result, except that we now need to apply the
test of internal coherence to the whole of 17 to make sure
that it might not have undergone serious rhapsodic expansion.
I believe it has not, that it is stylistically of a piece.
It is useful to recognise it as Homeric, and that tells us
something about his views on monumentality, about how far
one can go in developing a theme, about the function of
similes - in which 17 is particularly rich. But what we
shall learn if 5 is also by Homer is more surprising than
that.

First, though, consider the initial premise that 6 is
Homeric: is that really so axiomatic? After all, this is not
exactly an inescapable part of the large-scale plot. It is
artistically desirable (we might agree) that the Troy scenes
should take place, but one can imagine other ways in which,
for example, the character of Hector might have been
explored to increase the audience's involvement with him.
Book 6's Homeric claim rests rather on the almost unparalleled brilliance of the Trojan scenes. The most obvious
instance of that is so familiar that I hesitate to give it
even in summary. Everyone knows the scene in which Hector
finally tracks down his wife Andromache by the Scaean gate.
She has a nurse with her and their baby son Astyanax, who is
frightened by his father's great helmet-plume when Hector
tries to pick him up, so that both parents break the tension
by laughing. Suddenly we are carried into a softer and more
human world than that of ordinary heroic confrontation - but
are soon reminded that its values penetrate even there. For

when Hector takes off his helmet and places it shining on
the ground, he kisses the baby and dandles it and prays to
Zeus as follows: 'Grant that my son here may become like me
conspicuous among the Trojans, as physically strong and as
powerful a ruler over Ilios. Let the time come when it is
said "He is better than his father" as he returns from
battle; and may he carry bloody spoils after killing a foe-
man, and so rejoice his mother's heart' (476-81). Then back
to humanity: 'So saying he placed his child in his dear
wife's arms, and she took it into her fragrant bosom'
δακρυόεν γελάσασα, 'laughing tearfully'. They have already
discussed how things are, she imploring him to play safe, he
insisting on his responsibility to Troy but also on his love
for her; so Hector knows the cause of her tears and sends
her back to Troy ἐντροπαλιζομένη, continually turning to
look back at him.

No one who hears or reads that description can doubt the
poet's genius at this point - Homer's genius, that is, con-
centrated on the particular relation between Hector and
Andromache on that particular day in the tragic history of
Troy, a relation that is both tender and real, not possibly
just a great type-scene of warrior husband and faithful
wife. In theory, I suppose, there could have been an earlier
poem about a warrior coming back to a besieged city and
encountering various people there, and this might be part of
it; for the argument that 'what is brilliant must be by
Homer' can be misleading. But here we have brilliance, and a
quite unusual observation and understanding, applied to all
three of Hector's main meetings within the city, each of
them serving to prepare for one important part or another of
the monumental poem. First he meets his mother Hecabe -
indeed his immediate purpose is to tell her to organise
prayers to Athena to avert the crisis caused by Diomedes'
triumph. She behaves like a mother, urges him to rest and
take some refreshing wine, he makes a series of not very
good excuses because he wants to find Paris and get him back
into action. This he does in a stern and imposing meeting,
relieved by his sympathy for Helen who is also there; the
scene at the end of the third book where Aphrodite forced
Helen into bed with her consort, Paris, is marvellously
recaptured and extended, and both Helen and Hector emerge as
solider and more complex characters, which the monumental
plot badly needs them to be. Then Hector looks for Andromache, hurries through the streets to find her, is told she
is not at home, rushes back to the Scaean gate where she
dashes toward him. Thus the series of carefully planned
encounters reaches its brilliant climax, and Hector sallies
out of the city to return to the fighting, followed by his

erratic brother Paris, much revived now and prancing high
like a proud and excited stallion.

That this is all the monumental composer's work - his particular creation, though he uses many traditional elements,
much formulaic and thematic material derived from his predecessors - has not often been seriously doubted; although
some analysts were apt to see the whole of the block from 2
to the end of 7 as a separate development, secondary to the
main plot of the wrath of Achilles. That kind of analysis is
out of fashion now, and even then the unusual qualities of 6
were something of an embarrassment to those whose obsession
with major plot-elements prevented them from accepting it as
primarily Homeric. Let us at any rate have no such qualms,
for the sake of argument at least, and proceed with our
systematic investigation. Looking back to the beginning of
6, before Hector reaches Troy at verse 237, we might wonder
at first whether the monumental composer *is* so heavily
involved. Certainly there is more typical material here, to
do with the details of fighting in particular; and there is
the episode of Diomedes' meeting with Glaucus that looks
like a summary extract from a longer independent song. No
more than 115 verses elapse before Hector's departure for
Troy; they begin with the opening statement of the book that
Trojans and Achaeans are left to fight on their own, that is
without the intervention of gods - for 5 had ended with the
wounding and retreat of Ares and the withdrawal of Hera and
Athena on the Achaean side. Now comes a series of individual
encounters which interestingly enough follows the pattern,
though on a smaller scale, of those that opened Book 5 itself, and which shares with that book the taste for pairs of
victims (so that Diomedes kills Axylus and Calesius,
Euryalus kills Dresus and Opheltius, then Aesepus and
Pedasus, 6, 12-22).

Menelaus' combat with Adrestus, whom he inclines to spare
for ransom but then allows his reproachful brother Agamemnon
to slaughter, is told at greater length, and seems to have a
corresponding function (of breaking the sequence of small
encounters) to the wounding of Diomedes by Pandarus quite
early in Book 5. The Trojans are already in trouble again
(we need not worry over the apparent contradiction of Zeus'
promise to Thetis to drive the Achaeans back to the ships -
that works over a much longer time-scale), and that leads to
the reason for Hector's return to Troy. His brother Helenus
is a seer, and it is he that tells Hector and Aeneas to
rally the Trojan troops while Hector retires to the city to
get his mother to organise prayers and gifts for Athena, who
like Apollo is envisaged as having a temple in Troy. It is,
in truth, not a very strong piece of motivation, for Hector

is too crucial a figure to abandon his reeling troops at
this point, and indeed Helenus himself, an expert in religious matters, could presumably have done the job better. But
there are parallels elsewhere for perfunctory motivation in
the removal of a major character from one location to
another in order to introduce an important new scene; Ares
for example is removed from the battlefield with unrealistic
ease by Athena at 5, 29-36. Even the monumental composer
seems to be less than fully concerned with these points of
suture; he does not take pains to eradicate all signs of the
combining of major episodes from his existing repertoire in
the process of building up the large-scale epic; that is
something the writer would do, but which the oral performer
would perhaps not have the opportunity or even the motive to
perfect.

Hector, then, departs for Troy, and there follows the description of an intriguing and seemingly independent encounter between Glaucus and Diomedes. In one way it is part of
the *Diomedeia* , the *aristeia* or triumph of Diomedes; and
Herodotus quotes an extract from it as precisely from that
source. In another way it is one of those inorganic scenes
that could be inserted in the epic or omitted from it according to a poet's wishes - or even moved elsewhere as Aris-
tonicus reported to be the case with this particular episode.
On the whole I am inclined to believe that it is correctly
placed where it stands in Book 6, and that Homer developed
and adapted it to provide a tonal transition from fighting
to the tense but peaceful interviews in the city. At the
same time it makes a formal ending to Diomedes' interlude of
irresistible domination, summarises his confident heroism
through his own mouth, terminates his implied threats to the
gods, and through the heroic concept of *xenia* or guest-
friendship (which leads to the humorous or ironical climax
in which Glaucus is persuaded to exchange his expensive
armour for Diomedes' more ordinary set) extends the moral
issues of the siege beyond those of blow and counter-blow.
Thus although it is only the scenes inside Troy that are
undeniably Homeric in the fullest sense, those leading
directly up to them are consonant with the idea of special
attention being given by the monumental composer to the
whole of Book 6.

Book 5 is very different not only in subject (since all of
it takes place on the battlefield except for some closely
related scenes on Olympus) but also in style and what may be
termed realism. The Troy scenes of 6 are closely observed in
a psychological sense, and certainly contain nothing that
contradicts the ordinary rules and complexities of human
relations. Book 5, on the other hand, not only presents the

gods in their most anthropomorphic form but is also punctu-
ated by fantastic happenings that exceed the regular Homeric
conventions governing the relations of gods and men. The
result is that, although the *Diomedeia* taken as a whole
forms a justifiably dramatic component of the whole of the
first day's fighting, and has often therefore been placed in
a compositional unit formed by Books 2 or 3 to 7, it has
also been seen as a mixed composition, certainly not by
Homer, and combining archaic elements with many that are
dangerously new. Analysts have furthermore claimed to see a
decisive contradiction between 5 and the Glaucus and
Diomedes encounter in 6: 'one of the most glaring contradictions in the *Iliad*', as Walter Leaf put it, 'that between
the acts of Diomedes in 5 and his words in 6, 128'.[3] Let me
be rid of this objection without further delay. In the context of 6 Diomedes declares that he would on no account
fight with an immortal god, if that is what the ostensibly
unrecognised Glaucus happens to be. It is a half-humorous
statement in any case; but even if taken with deep solemnity
it reveals no real clash with Book 5, in which Diomedes was
given explicit permission by Athena to attack first Aphrodite, then (at 827 f.) Ares or any other god - for, she adds,
'you have in me such a supporter'. The Greek word for this
is ἐπιτάρροϑος, which judging from other Homeric uses means
a specific co-fighter on the battlefield, not a general
helper at all times or one that works, as a god might, from
far off. The point is that when Athena is not obviously at
Diomedes' side, visibly or invisibly, as she is throughout
his fight with Ares, then this promise and its encouragement
to take on all and sundry does not apply. At the end of 5
she leaves in company with Hera and they return to Olympus,
their mission accomplished; at the beginning of 6 the battle
is left free from divine interference, a change that must
have become soon apparent to the human participants; therefore Diomedes is fully justified in reverting to the ordinary rules of not attacking gods. If one likes to press
psychological implications one might add that he emphasises
this because of his consciousness of the remarkable feats
against deities that he has been allowed to get away with
shortly before.

Book 5 with 909 verses is the longest in the *Iliad*, and it
is important to recognise without delay that it is a highly
coherent stretch of narrative. It does not fall apart into
separable, inorganic or not entirely consistent episodes
which might have been accreted in a more or less mechanical
and therefore potentially rhapsodic manner. That kind of
thing can be observed in Book 8, for instance, where we
might be justified as seeing it not as the product of Homer

at his most creative, but at best of his working reproduc-
tively or under pressure, or perhaps even of relatively high-
grade rhapsodic elaboration. The different episodes of 5,
including the sequences of human battle-encounters, are
interwoven with each other as carefully as anywhere else in
the epic. Generally we expect to find a degree of looseness
in the alternating fortunes of battle and the almost routine
passage from victim to victim; but not only 8 (which is
rather an extreme case) but also 11 to 13, even, are less
tightly planned and executed than 5.

The book opens with Athena giving Diomedes special μένος
or might. Fire shines from his shield and helmet as he kills
one of a pair of brothers, Phegeus; the other has to be
rescued by Hephaestus. Ares is easily persuaded by Athena to
leave the field of battle, and six of the Achaean leaders
each pick off a victim who is carefully described, someone
out of the ordinary like Phereclus son of the Harmonides who
built the ship that took Paris on his fatal and adulterous
voyage. Diomedes meanwhile rages like a winter torrent, his
victims too numerous to distinguish, until Pandarus the
archer wounds him in the shoulder. Pandarus is soon to be
dealt with; now he boasts, thinking the shot to be fatal,
but Athena answers Diomedes' prayer to be enabled to fight
on; she tells him she has given him strength such as once
she gave to his father Tydeus, and bids him not to hesitate
to attack Aphrodite herself if she should enter the battle.
First he kills three pairs of victims, two of them brothers
- it is a favourite motif of this book. This rounds off the
small-scale fighting, for after 165 verses the poet seems to
feel that a longer episode is needed. So Aeneas, who figures
prominently in 5, searches out Pandarus to see if an arrow-
shot will stop Diomedes; Pandarus reports that he has
already tried and failed (it is typical of Homeric conventions that this is the end of the matter), and then the two
of them decide in a lengthy conversation to attack Diomedes
by chariot. Again there is a curious standard of realism:
Aeneas should surely never have entrusted his safety to an
untried spearsman like Pandarus, even if it might be prudent
to let his horses feel their master's touch on the reins.
Pandarus naturally succumbs in the encounter, and it is surprising that no reference is made at this point to the death
of the truce-breaker of Book 4. Aeneas' divine horses are
captured, but their owner is saved by his mother Aphrodite.

So Diomedes attacks the goddess and wounds her in the
wrist; she screeches and drops Aeneas (who is fielded by
Apollo) and is helped back to Olympus where she falls in her
mother's lap. Dione comforts her with a list of other crimes
of violence committed by men against gods. Meanwhile the

hero has attacked Apollo himself, and is only deterred on
the fourth attempt by the most serious warning. There are
closely similar passages in Books 21 and 16, especially the
latter (at 702 ff.); 16 is of course a key component in the
monumental plot, and it is interesting that 5 has several
detailed similarities to it. Ares is now summoned back by
Apollo to stiffen the Trojans, while Sarpedon rebukes Hector
and claims that too much is being left to the allies to do.
This 'rebuke pattern' always involves either Hector or
Aeneas and recurs several times in the *Iliad*, once in 16
again, once in the almost equally crucial 11, and no less
than four times in 17, which we saw to be a Homeric elaboration of the consequences of Patroclus' death in 16 - see
B.C. Fenik, *Typical Battle Scenes in the Iliad*,[4] pp.49 f.,
for all this. There is more to-and-fro fighting and then, to
vary the scale of action again, another developed individual
encounter, this time between Sarpedon and Tlepolemus. A further sequence of generic fighting provides a typical transition to the culminating episode of the book, occupying its
last 200 verses: the wounding of Ares. It begins when Hera
and Athena can no longer stand watching their chosen instru-
ment Diomedes being frustrated by Ares and Apollo. After a
wonderful scene in which they arm for battle and prepare
their chariot they call on Zeus and obtain his permission to
intervene, then descend to the plain of Troy, conceal their
chariot in a mist, and advance like strutting doves - a surprising and effective simile - until Hera briefly assumes
the form of Stentor to rally the Achaeans, and Athena
revives Diomedes by once again assuaging his shoulder-wound
and, like Agamemnon in 4, comparing him unfavourably and
quite unfairly with his father Tydeus at Thebes. Not only
does she encourage him to attack Ares, she actually dis-
places Sthenelos as charioteer and takes her place at his
side, so that the axle creaks under the weight of such a god
and such a hero. Ares is discovered plundering a warrior he
has slain - a remarkable and unparalleled action for a
Homeric god. Athena diverts his spear-thrust and directs
Diomedes' counter-thrust into the god's belly; he roars with
pain, as loud as nine or ten thousand men, and rushes up
into the sky like a whirlwind or something similar (864-7).
He droops fainting before Zeus and complains about his
attacker, just as Aphrodite had done to Dione; Zeus rebukes
him (for this is a despicable god who represents war in its
worst aspects) but has Apollo heal the wound, since Ares is,
after all, Zeus' own son. And so the book ends with the god
restored and complacent and the two goddesses returning home
to Olympus, their immediate task of relieving the Achaeans
and punishing their divine enemies accomplished - except of

course for Apollo, who cannot be treated so lightly.

No summary can demonstrate the careful coherence of this long and enthralling fifth book, but I hope to have given a fair indication of it. The alternation of detailed and generic descriptions of fighting, of condensed and extended narrative, of human and divine focus, of Diomedes and other warriors, and above all of Achaean and Trojan and then Achaean predominance again, has been lovingly and effectively carried through. Certain other qualities beyond those of unified planning must have made themselves felt, not least the unusual and fantastic turns of events, and I shall return to these shortly; but first I want to complete the record of cross-links with 6, our most completely Homeric datum, and also with 4. Here are the significant themes common to 5 and 6: the patterning of initial fighting in each book; Tydeus, who extends from Agamemnon's inspection in 4 through 5 to make a final brief appearance in the Diomedes and Glaucus conversation at 6, 222 f.; Aeneas, who is rather gratuitously associated with Hector at 6, 75 ff., presumably because of his prominence on the Trojan side in 5; the role of Diomedes himself, which extends from 5 backward into 4 and forward into the Glaucus episode in 6; the taste for older tales (Dione's list of divine sufferings at 5, 383-415 and the story of Bellerophon at 6, 155-206); and even such details as Hector's taciturnity to Sarpedon at 5, 689 and to Paris at 6, 342. As for 4, the main connexions not already mentioned are Hera and Athena getting Zeus' permission to intervene (4, 1-104 and 5, 711 ff. - slightly differently, to be sure); non-fatal wounds from Pandarus' arrows (on Menelaus in 4, Diomedes in 5); and the unjust rebuking of Diomedes (by Agamemnon at 4, 365-418 and by Athena at 5, 800-13) met by extraordinary patience on his part.

These connexions between 4 and 5 and 5 and 6 are extended by important points in common between 4 and 6 themselves. The Lycian ambush set for Bellerophon in Glaucus' tale at 6, 187-90 is closely parallel (including verbally: 6, 187 and 4, 392) to the ambush set for Tydeus by the Thebans at 4, 391-8, and in the last of these verses comes the striking phrase θεῶν τεράεσσι πιθήσας, which recurs literally only at 6, 183. Nestor's tactical wisdom, but here without long reminiscence attached, appears both at 4, 293-310 and at 6, 66-71; and the striking formula ταῦτα (τὰ) δ' ὄπισθεν ἀρεσσόμεθ' is unique to these books, at 4, 362 and 6, 526. These examples could be extended, as could wider contacts between what begins to look like a Homeric nucleus and its outlying episodes; especially with Book 3 (where Helen's attitude to Paris at 408-36 is parallel to and complemented

by that at 6, 349-58, and where Aphrodite's rescue of Paris
is paralleled by her rescue of Aeneas in 5) and even with
much of Book 7 (where Nestor's interest in the dead on the
battlefield at 6, 68-70 is reflected in the different concern at 7, 327 ff., where Helenus plays a similar role at
44 f. to that at 6, 75 f., and where Athena leads Apollo off
the battlefield at 20-42 as easily as she had led Ares away
at 5, 29-37). Books 3 and 7 are themselves thematically connected, of course, by the rather unexpected re-development
in 7 of the formal duel theme already elaborated in 3.

It would not be surprising in itself, even for those who
do not hold a wholly unitarian view of composition, if virtually all the events of the first day's fighting, from the
march-out in 2 (leaving aside the exact status of the
Achaean and Trojan catalogues) to nightfall at the end of 7,
were not only part of Homer's large-scale plan but also contained much of his own special work; and the detailed connexions I have just adduced provide a degree of positive
confirmation. Most of these connexions have, of course, been
often noticed before (though every critic assigns his own
particular weight to each of them), and mainly by analysts.
One of the latest developments in the merry-go-round of
Homeric scholarship is the need to return to arguments that
are essentially analytical ones, even now and in the wake of
oral studies and hard or soft Milman Parry-ism. For the
truth is that anyone who closely studies the text of either
Iliad or *Odyssey* to see how it works ends up by relating
theme to theme and episode to episode. He may do so against
a background of assumptions about mechanical processes of
composition by a limited sequence of authors, as the analysts did; or his assumption may be that of an only partly
penetrable tradition of oral poets such as we might accept
from Parry. But we are dealing in each case with the same
connexions, repetitions and apparent inconcinnities, and it
is salutary to see how much can still be learnt from early
twentieth century German critics like Rothe and Drerup.

After that mild dose of corrective medicine I return to
the special relations of 5 and 6 and leave the wider links
on one side. For if 6 is certainly substantially by Homer,
and 5, which is a closely integrated whole, is essentially
linked with 6, then 5 is also Homeric in the fullest sense.
Let us assume that to have been proved, for the sake of
argument at least, and see what follows. The most important
conclusion will concern some supposedly odd characteristics
of 5 at which I have barely hinted so far; some of them will
turn out on inspection to be fictitious, others will be real
but will perhaps have causes and implications quite different from those fondly placed on them by our old analyst

friends.

The first of the oddities is not so much the supposed *inconsistency* of Diomedes' attitude to attacking gods (for this, as I showed, only applied to the relation between 5 and 6, and in any case was in the end non-existent) as the idea of such attacks in itself. But it is certainly not a novel one, since Patroclus tries to attack Apollo at 16, 700-9 just as Diomedes does at 5, 432-42, and in quite similar terms. I have already noted that Patroclus' role in 16 is particularly Homeric. The actual wounding of gods by a mortal is indeed unique in the action of the *Iliad*, but Dione's list of physical acts of violence against gods at 5, 385 ff. shows that this sort of thing was part of the tradition - although perhaps not of its specifically Trojan sector. The reason why the monumental poet chose to develop the idea in 5 and not elsewhere cannot be precisely defined, but several probable factors present themselves: that in this early part of the poem he is concerned with exploiting all sorts of exotic themes as a means of delaying the next stage in the consequences of Achilles' wrath - themes like the long catalogues in 2, the viewing from the walls and the formal duel in 3, the inspection of his troops by Agamemnon in 4, the Troy-scenes in 6, the repeated formal duel and the gathering of the dead in 7. None of these are typical Homeric themes, and some of them are used without the strongest regard for chronological appropriateness or the avoidance of major repetition. The *aristeia* of Diomedes in 5 may itself be regarded as such a large-scale interruption of the action, although it does at least continue the actual fighting. But its dominant motif is certainly that of Diomedes' attacks on the gods that stand in his way, under the active support of Athena, and it is this that is the special, exotic contribution of the fifth book - one that can now be seen as parallel to other untypical features in the surrounding books, features which may nevertheless be perfectly in accord with the plan of the monumental poem.

Secondly, there are scattered through Book 5 several untypical and almost miraculous details or events which are strange to the style of the poem as a whole, though not altogether unparalleled. Ares leans his spear and chariot against a cloud (355 f.), gods are said to have a special substance called *ichōr* in their veins (339, 416), Apollo makes an *eidōlon* or image of Aeneas (449), Athena has actual weight and makes the axle creak (837-9), Ares kills Periphas and loots his armour like the most concrete of mortal warriors (841 f., 846-8), he shouts as loudly when wounded as nine or ten thousand men (859-61), and Athena puts on a cap of invisibility to direct Diomedes' spear (844). These are

all concerned with the gods, but there is one *phantasma* (to
use a modern technical term) that is absolutely secular; for
when the charioteer Mydon is fatally wounded by Antilochus
at 580-9 he falls out of the chariot head first into soft
sand and sticks there, feet in the air, until the horses
knock him over. Such bizarre deaths are not absolutely unparalleled elsewhere in the poem, and once again one is sent
first and foremost to Book 16, where Patroclus lifts his
victim out of the chariot by the end of his spear like a
fish on the end of a line. Finally one of the few similes in
our fifth book is impressive but almost unintelligible, when
'like dark mist that appears from clouds after heat, when a
harsh wind arises, so did brazen Ares appear to Diomedes as
he went to the broad sky accompanied by clouds' (864-7).
Certainly this does not reveal Homer's customary clarity of
vision and expression in the developed similes; but just as
Ares' wounding is practically unique, so he may choose an
unusual phenomenon to illustrate it, and that is where the
strain arises.
   Beyond the details of the behaviour of gods, especially
Ares and Aphrodite, the famous peculiarities of Book 5 turn
out to amount to very little. Nearly all the divine elements,
moreover, arise out of the poet's evident desire to make the
gods appear as like mortals as possible in their behaviour,
once he has decided to develop the theme of Diomedes wounding them as the distinguishing feature of his triumph. Some
critics have even found it difficult that the wounding of
Ares is obviously so closely parallel to that of Aphrodite;
but this kind of repeated use of a theme, with careful vari-
ation on the second occasion, is typical of the oral style
as well as being dramatically effective in the present case
- more so, it must be admitted, than the repetition in 7 of
the formal-duel theme of 3. Odd and unique details appear
from time to time throughout the epic, not least in the most
obviously Homeric parts of it. Admittedly the rhapsodes'
preference for essential components like *Iliad*, Book 1 meant
that they left their mark even there - but usually in the
form of strained expansions recognisable by their language
rather than by wholly untypical additions. It is a false
taste that reveals everything unusual as 'late' in the sense
of post-Homeric. Some people have even felt that about the
developed similes in general, and they have been encouraged
by G.P. Shipp's demonstration that the similes, like other
digressions, contain a higher than usual proportion of relatively late forms.[5] But 'relatively late' means precisely
'by Homer' in this case - because Homer did, of course,
demonstrably come at the end of the oral tradition; and I
wonder whether the divine peculiarities of Book 5 are not

also a special mark of his imagination extending into
regions that were not entirely new, but were normally more
concerned with Heracles, for example, than with Troy.

One particularly nice peculiarity in my judgement is that
idea, confined to this book and to the wounding of Aphrodite,
that the gods have ἰχώρ (later to mean 'serum') in their
veins, not blood: 'immortal blood of the goddess flowed,
ichōr, such as flows for blessed gods; for they do not eat
human food nor drink gleaming wine, and for that reason they
are bloodless and are called immortal' (339-42). Despite its
scholarly and aetiological tone, that looks too clever to be
rhapsodic elaboration. Admittedly, if it is Homer's own idea,
it might seem surprising that he did not refer to it elsewhere; but it is only in this book that divine blood is
likely to flow at all, and repetition in the case of Ares
might have seemed too obvious. But it accords interestingly
with a process that I believe can be traced here and there
in the Homeric poems and which forms part of what I term the
spiritualisation of the Olympian gods. Of course that is an
erratic affair, and Hera's *avoirdupois* can be mentioned in
the same broad context as Aphrodite's *ichōr*; but still there
seems to be a change in the air over the way gods were conceived, from meat-eaters (at the time when men still ban-
queted with them, in mythical terms) to meat-savour-sniffers
(the common Iliadic picture of gods enjoying κνίση or the
smoke of burning fat from sacrifices below) to consumers
only of ambrosia and nectar. The idea of them as bloodless
(and by implication of blood as the life-giving substance
for men) is a neat extension of this last stage. But that is
a different topic which I must pursue elsewhere; and I
return to the conclusion that Book 5 is Homeric, that
details which we might be inclined to assign to rhapsodic
elaboration or other kinds of later expansion are few indeed,
and that acceptance of such a contention enormously enlarges
our idea of Homer's own range of style and tastes.

But Homeric criticism can never be quite as simple as that.
For every time one reaches a conclusion about the mode in
which a section of the *Iliad* was composed - about its relation to other parts of the text, in less rigid terms - one
has to remind oneself of a dozen other passages that are almost as clear-cut, that have many characteristics in common,
but that point to a quite different conclusion. That is the
result of the pervasive traditional constituent of the poems,
and the subtle and often un-reconstructable ways in which a
singer, especially a highly creative one like Homer himself,
works upon his traditional material. For Book 5 we have just
such a quasi-parallel to hand; for the Theomachy or Battle
of the Gods which begins and is then abruptly abandoned in

Book 20, to be resuscitated and brought to an unsatisfactor-
ily burlesque conclusion in 21, has several points in common
with Diomedes' wounding of gods in 5. Artemis, for example,
is whipped with her own bow and arrows by Hera and retreats
to be comforted by Zeus (21, 479-513), which presents obvious
similarities to Aphrodite in 5. Is the Theomachy, then, to
be rated as a further exercise by Homer himself, in which he
takes the relative innovations of 5 a step too far? Or is it
an imitative elaboration of 5 developed by some follower or
rhapsode? Or were both episodes there in the tradition in
embryo, to be developed independently and applied with dif-
fering success by the monumental composer? My own feeling is
that the second of these, somewhat qualified, is closer to
the truth than the others - that Homer may have begun to
describe a general quarrel among the gods, but that much of
the version in our text (not least the Hesiodic-sounding
description of cosmic repercussions) is a tasteless expansion by followers: one of the very few in the whole poem. In
any case the total effect, with its clear signs of mechanical manipulation and displacement, is very different from
that of complete coherence in 5.

The Theomachy reminds us to be cautious, therefore; it
shows once again how complex is the process of composition
in an oral tradition, even more so in one that was then sub-
jected to a period of semi-literate transmission. But the
Troy-scenes of Book 6, taken together with his handling of
the deaths of Patroclus and Hector later in the poem, are
clear proof of Homer's versatility as well as his genius;
and the triumph of Diomedes in 5 seems to extend his range
still further.

NOTES

1. A.B. Lord, *The Singer of Tales* (Cambridge, Mass., 1960);
   R. Finnegan, *Oral Poetry* (Cambridge, 1977).
2. In *Homer and the Oral Tradition* (Cambridge, 1976) pp.201-
   17.
3. *The Iliad*, 2nd edn (London, 1900) vol.1, p.192.
4. Wiesbaden, 1968.
5. *Studies in the Language of Homer* (Cambridge, 1953).

3 Homeric Epic and the Tragic Moment

JOHN GOULD

My subject in this paper is the response of the tragic poets
of fifth-century Athens to the Homeric epics, and beyond
that, the meaning that the Homeric poems had for their audience in the fifth century. It is a subject which is going,
inevitably, to raise a certain number of puzzles and paradoxes, one or two of which I shall try to throw some light
on. But there is one, which must surely arise sooner or
later, which I can deal with only by confessing at the out-
set that I have nothing as yet to say about it - unless this
whole paper can be taken as a comment upon it. Which is, no
doubt, a confession of serious failure, since we are concerned, on the face of it, with one of the few pieces of
contemporary evidence that we have, and it comes (or pur-
ports to come) from no less a witness than Aeschylus himself.
Evidently these are words which must prove invaluable. But I
do not know what they mean. They form a remark of Aeschylus
alluded to in passing rather than quoted in the interminably
allusive conversation that makes up Athenaeus' *Table-talk*
(8.347e). The subject of this particular stretch of talk is
cooking and eating fish, and one of the talkers, apropos of
not leaving the biggest and best cuts in order to pick over
bone and gristle, refers to 'Aeschylus' saying, that his
plays were cuts from the great banquets of Homer. That's it:
no context, no explanation, and above all, no examples;
nothing more than a quite generalised implication of
Aeschylus' indebtedness to the Homeric poems, of his consciousness of obligation. It is hard even to be sure whether
the word that I have translated 'cuts' implies choice por-
tions or mere scraps. And if we ask 'what kind of debt?' and
'to what poems?', we have next to no evidence for a direct
answer. We can only guess which poems Aeschylus would have
called Homer's, and if we look at the surviving fragments
and titles that are all we have of Aeschylus' huge output

beyond the seven (or should it be six?) extant plays, we
shall be hard put to it to find more than three or four that
take their subject matter from the *Odyssey* or *Iliad*, and
another ten or eleven that might perhaps derive from episodes found in other poems of the Trojan cycle: that is, at
most, fifteen plays which might owe something of their
origin to 'Homeric' poems in the widest possible sense, out
of between eighty and ninety plays attested. The picture is
hardly different if we look at what we know of the plays of
Sophocles and Euripides. The debt, then, it seems is not one
which involves the derivation of stories or plot material.

Nor is it one marked by giving the language of tragedy an
epic colouring. True, there are echoes from time to time of
Homeric phraseology, occasionally of Homeric syntax. But
these are sporadic and for the most part specific reminiscences of Homeric language in a particular context and for
particular effect. They are altogether different from the
consistently epic colouring of the language of Greek elegy,
for example, or of the 'abnormal' poems of Sappho, and still
further removed from the *epyllia* of Theocritus: these,
clearly, set out to evoke the tenor of epic poetry through
their language in a way which is quite alien to Greek
tragedy. And this is not, of course, because tragedy uses
only the vernacular of fifth-century Attica in any way which
excludes the evocation of an alien tone. The 'Doric' colouring of the lyrics of tragedy provides a continuous reminder
that tragedy acknowledges connexions with worlds other than
that of contemporary Athens. It will not do, here, to point
to alleged 'epic' features of the language of messenger
speeches (the omitted syllabic augment and avoidance of the
definite article), since not only are these best explained
in other ways (given the almost total absence, for example,
of epic vocalisation or morphology), but restricted as they
are to messenger speeches and to a handful only of these,
they can hardly in themselves constitute an implication of
tragedy's whole debt to Homeric epic.

Perhaps, then, a matter, more generally, of example, of
being in Homer's debt for the imaginative projection of a
world in which human action is given a scale, a moral complexity and a seriousness that matched the needs of the
fifth-century tragic dramatists? That at least would make
some sense of Aeschylus' purported remark. But at first
sight, at least, there are obvious obstacles in the way of
adopting such a view, the most immediately significant of
which is indicated in my title. We have, after all, learnt
over the past two or three decades to think of the consciousness of fifth-century Greece, and above all of Athens in the
fifth century, as something radically different from that of

earlier centuries, and to think of tragedy in particular as
the characteristic expression of that new consciousness. I
mean what Jean-Pierre Vernant and others have called 'le
moment tragique' and all that is implied in that phrase.

The thesis, briefly, is this. The development in new forms
of social organisation and in new political institutions
that marks the transition from the 'archaic' world of the
seventh and sixth centuries to the 'new' societies of fifth-
century Greece, and above all that of democratic Athens,
accompanied by the gradual spread of literacy in the Greek
world, brought about a shift of consciousness, a new spirit
of rational and critical enquiry, a new readiness, even a
compelling need, to re-examine and to attack traditional
assumptions that brought the societies of ancient Greece
(and again Athens is the prime example) across the divide
that students of social development such as Jack Goody see
as separating 'traditional' from 'modern', 'primitive' from
'advanced', 'cold' from 'hot'. The experience of open discussion of fundamental assumptions about society and about
political and legal decision-making had created in men a
radical and a cumulative scepticism about traditional wisdom
and a new sophistication in the analysis of human behaviour
and motivation. Added to this, it is argued, comes an increasing awareness of, and in some Greeks at least, a con-
suming interest in the varieties of human experience and of
human solutions to the problems of experience, all of which
leads to a new world-outlook. Now if we look, however cur-
sorily, at the life-span of Aeschylus, for example, we can
hardly find grounds to doubt the factual premises at least
of the argument that the world in which he died (in 456 B.C.)
was in very many respects a wholly different world from that
in which he was born, in 525 B.C. or thereabouts. Then the
sons of Peisistratus still held power in Athens: by his
death Aeschylus had lived through the ending of the Peisis-
tratid tyranny by Spartan intervention, the reforms of
Cleisthenes, the introduction of ostracism, the building of
the Long Walls, the Persian invasions of Darius and Xerxes
and the great expansion of Athenian power and prestige in
the Aegean that followed, and the process, culminating in
the removal from the Areopagus of its traditional powers and
the assassination of Ephialtes, that established in Athens
the most radical democracy in Greece and brought Pericles
(who had been Aeschylus' *choregos* for the production of
Persians in 472 B.C.) to the beginning of a political ascen-
dancy that was to last for more than twenty years. It would
be hardly surprising if Aeschylus, and a fortiori his suc-
cessors in the Athenian theatre, found it hard to share the
assumptions that had seemed self-evident to his great-

grandfather, and the birth of tragedy, the 'tragic moment',
is the product and expression of this new sense of things,
of debate and doubt and conflict over the belief-system of
ancient Greeks.

The thesis, thus described, is evidently a matter of hypo-
thesis and speculation, not of demonstration, and one which,
in the over-simple terms in which I have described it, is
all too obviously open to objections both of detail and of
substance. But I am confirmed in thinking that the thesis is
far from being altogether mistaken by the re-examination
lately given to it, in the somewhat different but related
context of the rise of scientific thought in ancient Greece,
by Geoffrey Lloyd in his book *Magic, Reason and Experience*.[1]
With admirable discrimination and precision, with great
learning and with judicious use of the analogies provided
both by anthropological studies of intellectual change in
primitive societies and by the history of the great riverine
cultures of the ancient Near East, he has succeeded both in
significantly refining the thesis and in dealing seriously
with some of the most important prima facie objections to it.
He concludes that the decisive factors in bringing about the
intellectual changes which he documents were not technologi-
cal or economic development, nor even the spread of alpha-
betic literacy, but lay 'in the development of a particular
social and political situation in ancient Greece, especially
the experience of radical political debate and confrontation
in small-scale, face-to-face societies' (p.266).

Such, then, is the thesis of the 'tragic moment'. Its
relevance to my subject in this paper is clear enough. If it
is true that social and political change had, by the time of
Aeschylus, brought about a radical break with many fundamental strands in traditional thinking about human experience,
should we not expect to find that in Aeschylus and his suc-
cessors an image is presented of the human condition that
differs toto caelo from that presented in the Homeric poems,
and that correspondingly the Homeric poems have come to be
seen as belonging to an alien past and as offering a model
of man's existence that by its very distance from contemporary reality had little to say to the 'new' men of the fifth
century?

The first of these expectations is, at first glance at
least, confirmed by what we find in fifth-century tragedy.
The world of political debate, of the free and open clash of
opinion before a mass assembly, and of decision by vote and
not by acclamation in such an assembly, if for the most part
it remains off-stage, none the less begins to invade the
imagined world of the Greek tragic theatre as early as
Aeschylus' *Suppliant Women* in the 460s: the Argive king

refuses either to accept or to reject the plea of Danaus'
daughters for protection as suppliants 'without the people',
for fear of what 'the mass (the λεώς)' might say of him if
any disaster should ensue (397 ff.) and later 'persuasion
attends' his words, and the people vote, in language that
precisely evokes the language of decisions of the Athenian
assembly, with 'the air quivering with a forest of right
hands' (650 ff.), to accept the suppliants as resident
aliens (Μέτοικοι) and to give them sanctuary (ἀσυλία). Contemporary language and a contemporary image of political
decision that belongs to another world from the Iliadic
world in which Agamemnon can send Chryses away with threats
and abuse 'harshly . . . with a strong order upon him', for
all that 'all the rest of the Achaeans' had 'cried out in
favour' of his plea (Il., 1. 22-5): Agamemnon's authority at
this moment is absolute.

In *Prometheus*, which, even if it is not the work of
Aeschylus, is none the less a product of fifth-century 'en-
lightenment', the accession of Zeus to power is imagined,
not on the Hesiodic model of a son displacing his father,
according to a pattern which was repeated from one generation to another, but as the overthrow of one power-holding
clan by another, that is through the political model of the
establishment of a tyranny and the ousting of an earlier
aristocracy: Zeus is the young tyrant who has just seized an
arbitrary power with the backing of his kinsmen and whose
'court' (αὐλή) is thronged by lesser gods who owe their
powers and privileges (γέρα: *P.V.* 228 ff.) to him, but whose
own power and sway (ἀρχή,σκῆπτρον and τιμαί: *P.V.* 165 ff.)
are vulnerable to further attempts to seize it from him by
force. The image is one drawn from contemporary political
experience of *stasis* (the word is used of conflict among the
gods at *P.V.* 200), and it has a political sophistication to
it that is once more foreign to the world of the Homeric
poems.

In line with this, we cannot be surprised if the image of
warfare that we find in the plays of Aeschylus seems very
different from the Iliadic image. Not just in the presentation of actual contemporary experience of war in *Persians*,
but even in the imagined experience of the great subject of
Homeric epic, war at Troy, in *Agamemnon*. War in this play is
imaged first in mourning and bitterness at home: 'in place
of men . . . an urn and ashes', which Ares the money-changer
of the dead bodies of men ships home, 'packing jars with a
man's worth of ashes, easy to handle'; the fighting 'for
another man's wife', 'a woman of many men', is resented in
silence and muttered words, and 'heavy is the murmur of an
angry citizenry: it demands payment for a people's curse'

(*Agam.*, 433-57). When we hear in this play from one who has
fought at Troy, we hear not of heroic encounters and heroic
death, but of the miseries of conditions at Troy for the
mass of men who fought: 'our beds lay under the enemies'
walls; drizzle from the sky and from the earth marsh-dews,
unending, filling our clothes and hair with lice'. Intoler-
able winters that killed even the birds, and summer heat,
'when the sea in its noon sleep falls drowsy, waveless and
windless' (*Agam.*, 559-67). It is an experience best forgot-
ten, outbalanced only by the glory and the proud boast of
having taken Troy: it is a sombre and unheroic picture which,
once more, owes more to contemporary experience of war, it
seems, than to the model of Homeric epic.

   If now we turn to the central issue, the issue of the
moral implications of human experience, we seem to see again
a striking difference between the moral assumptions of the
Homeric poems and those of fifth-century tragedy. The case
of Agamemnon's murder and of the revenge of Orestes is an
obvious point of comparison. The story of how Agamemnon came
home from Troy and was murdered by his cousin Aegisthus with
the connivance of Clytaemnestra, his wife, and how his son
Orestes avenged that murder runs as a recurring theme
through the first half of the *Odyssey*, and it is, of course,
the subject of plays by all three of the fifth-century dramatists. The story is first mentioned in the dialogue of the
gods at the beginning of the first book of the *Odyssey*; it
is referred to again by the disguised Athena talking to
Telemachus later in the same book; referred to and then told
at length by Nestor to Telemachus in Book three; told again
to Telemachus by Menelaus in Book four, and finally by the
ghost of Agamemnon to Odysseus in the eleventh book. In
every case except the last (where for obvious reasons Agamemnon does not know the outcome) the story culminates in
Orestes' revenge, and in each case the act of Orestes is
presented as a paradigm to Telemachus of the behaviour of
the dutiful son. The moral implications of the story are
drawn out as clear-cut and unambiguous. Orestes' action is
to be a stimulus to Telemachus to acknowledge that he is now
of age and must meet his obligations: 'have you not heard
what glory (κλέος) great Orestes won among all men, when he
killed his father's murderer . . . ? Be bold, you also, so
that in generations to come men may praise you' (*Od.*, 1. 298-
302). Contrast with this the central significance of Orestes'
revenge in fifth-century drama as moral paradox: 'you killed
whom you should not: now suffer what you should not', says
Aeschylus' Orestes to the mother he is about to kill
(*Choeph.*, 930), and the Dioscuri in Euripides' *Electra* say
to Orestes; 'she [the dead Clytaemnestra] has now what is

right, but what you do is wrong' (*El.*, 1244). It is of the
essence, indeed it constitutes perhaps the whole fascination
of the Orestes story for the fifth-century dramatists that
it does *not* offer any unambiguous moral to a contemporary
audience, but rather contradiction and ambivalence, that it
provides the matter for conflicting interpretation, for
argument and dissent, even for doubting the wisdom of the
gods who approved it and for the self-doubt of Orestes.

The Orestes story as it is dramatised in the fifth-century
theatre involves a radical re-casting even of the basic data
that are given in the *Odyssey*. In place of a story of male
seduction of an at first unwilling wife and perhaps of
family feud between cousins, Aeschylus gives us in *Agamemnon*
and *Choephoroe* an action in which sex-roles are reversed and
familial relationships denied; in which the man-woman
Clytaemnestra plots her husband's death with a demonic sense
of power and mastery, while the man Aegisthus, who can be
called 'woman' by the chorus, arrives after the slaughter is
done, devoid of authority or dramatic significance: the
world of *Agamemnon* is a world reversed, which abounds in
images of the fertility of evil and of a terrible sickness
in human relations. Something of the same sombre reshaping
of Homeric material can be seen in another play which makes
striking but disturbing use of motifs drawn from the *Iliad*.

Sophocles' *Ajax*, more than any other extant Greek play,
recalls specific moments of the *Iliad* with an unmistakeable
and ironic intensity, as well as giving us, in Odysseus, a
character who clearly derives from the Odysseus of the
second half of the *Odyssey*, conscious of mutability and of
the precariousness of human achievement (*Ajax*, 121-6: cf.
Od., 18. 129 ff.). But in recalling Homeric precedent,
Sophocles conspicuously adjusts what he takes over to render
new meanings from these echoes of epic scenes. In the scene
between Ajax and Tecmessa, in which she appeals to him, now
returned to sanity after his mad assault on the cattle, to
turn aside from thoughts of suicide and not to abandon her
and her son by him to the humiliation of mockery as the
slave of his enemies, Sophocles insistently evokes the scene
in *Iliad*, 6 between Hector and Andromache, one of the great
moments in Homeric epic. But the echoes are distorted: as
well as echoing the language of Andromache's lament for her
lost father and brothers, Tecmessa uses language which in
Homer belongs, not to Andromache, but to Hector, words which
in the *Iliad* make overpoweringly real to us Hector's moving
response to Andromache's plea. But in Sophocles Ajax is not
moved: he is tight-lipped and curt, and ruthlessly shuts
himself away from the possibility of any response to Tecmessa's words. The encounter between father and son which

follows again recalls Hector's bitter-sweet moments with *his*
infant son, Astyanax, and again with such distortion of the
echo that the effect is of a coarsening and brutalising of
the idea of heroic action. 'You must break him in, now,'
Ajax says to Tecmessa, 'to his father's raw ways' (ὠμοῖς . . .
ἐν νόμοις πατρός (*Ajax*, 548-9)): 'raw' is not a word Homer
uses of Hector, or of Ajax, but only of the 'eaters of raw
flesh', jackals, wolves, lions, dogs, birds and fish, and in
metaphor of the inhuman, implacable hatred of Troy by Hera,
or of Hector by Achilles; it is used three more times of
Ajax in Sophocles' play. Again, in the sword that is the
means of Ajax' suicide, Sophocles recalls the exchange of
gifts that ends the duel between Hector and Ajax in *Iliad*, 7
(7.299 ff.), gifts which in Homer were to make men say
'These men fought each other in heart-consuming hate, then/
joined with each other in close friendship, before they were
parted.' In Sophocles the sword of Hector is 'the butcher',
a malign talisman which only recalls to Ajax the man 'most
loathed of all I know, most hated to my sight', a gift that
evokes the proverb 'the gifts of enemies are no gifts and
bring no benefit', whose 'true goodwill' to Ajax consists in
bringing him a swift death. Its counterpart, the belt that
Ajax gave to Hector, is remembered by Ajax as the very belt
with which Achilles tied him to his chariot rail and dragged
him, still living, until he died 'carded on the stones'
(*Ajax*, 1024 ff.): another alteration to Homeric precedent
which makes the death of Hector also shockingly more igno-
minious and more brutal.

In this way, some of the bright and human moments of heroic encounter in the *Iliad* are given by Sophocles a strikingly more sombre, starker, even bitter colouring in his echoing of them. Yet Sophocles does not mean to make of Ajax
merely a brutal killer: even if, as Professor Winnington-
Ingram has suggested, he is 'one who carries the implications of the heroic code to the extreme possible point, as
no one in Homer . . . ever did',[2] still there is a nobility
in Ajax' language, a strength and constancy, that is unmistakeable, as well as a haunting sense of affinity with the
very scenes of heroic conflict before Troy, the rivers and
beaches of the Iliadic scene, that gives his heroism a human
quality not in the last resort so alien to the Homeric hero.
For however much it is true that the relation of fifth-
century theatre to the world of Homeric epic is repeatedly
an ironic and ambiguous one, still we should be all too obviously wrong to conclude that the heroic imagery of Homeric
epic could not be handled by the fifth-century dramatists
except ironically and was without directly accessible
meaning to fifth-century audiences. For proof, we have only

to turn to Plato's account of the reception of Ion's per-
formances of Homer on a contemporary audience (*Ion*, 535b-e)
or to the speech that Plato wrote to convey his sense of
Socrates' defence in his trial in 399 B.C. In the *Apology*,
Plato makes Socrates cite the example precisely of Achilles,
and more generally of the Greek heroes who died at Troy, for
the proposition that the certainty of death is to be treated
as having no weight in the balance against dishonour: the
Achilles who preferred to bring about his own death rather
than be mocked as one who 'sits here beside my ships, a use-
less weight on the good land' has still a clear significance
for fifth-century Athenians, unobscured by reservations or
by ironical reflection (*Apol.*, 28b-d).

If we ask 'how so?', in the light of how much had changed
to separate the world of fifth-century Athens from that of
Homer, a large part of the answer must lie in what had *not*
changed, in the continuities of a moral code that, before
Socrates at least, had maintained its hold to a degree that
must often surprise us if we give too much weight or allow
too much scope to the fundamentally correct assumption of
radical change in belief-systems. It is not just that, as
Geoffrey Lloyd has pointed out, traditional patterns of
belief persist widely and at all levels of society in spite
of all attacks upon such beliefs, but also that the continuing use of a model of human relationships which sees conflict, reciprocal aggression, the defence of honour and the
urge to vengeance as fundamental human traits made it possible to read the experience of Achilles in the *Iliad* as no
less paradeigmatic in the fifth century than in the seventh
or eighth. Conflict in the *Iliad* has as its central image
the armed conflict of heroes, but it is none the less an
intelligible metaphor of human experience for a fifth-
century Athenian. The Ajax of Sophocles' play is in one
sense an archaic, outmoded figure when contrasted with the
more 'modern' Odysseus, but in another perspective an image
of an absolute 'morality of honour' which had lost nothing
of its relevance for the contemporaries of Alcibiades.

But there is, I think, more to it than that. When we think
of the *Iliad* and *Odyssey* as traditional poems, as 'heroic
poetry' preserving a traditional image of human existence,
we are liable to blind ourselves to what Oliver Taplin has
called their 'intricacy', the 'modernity' of their vision of
man, and the complexity, rather than simplicity, of their
imagined world. We think, for example, (and rightly) of a
passion for argument and an excited connoisseurship of fertility, ingenuity and sophistication in the presentation of an
argument as typical features of fifth-century Athenian culture. The enthusiasm for rhetorical skills which we find in

the writings of Gorgias or in Antiphon's *Tetralogies*, and
which Thucydides' Cleon detected in the approach of the
fifth-century assembly to political debate is, we would say,
a characteristic feature of the Athens of the mid-fifth century. But a dozen years ago Kenneth Dover pointed out
(*Lysias and the Corpus Lysiacum*,[3] pp.176-8) that the description in *Iliad*, 3 of Menelaus and Odysseus addressing the
assembled Trojans is the work of a connoisseur of rhetorical
speech-making, and that the account of the quarrel between
Agamemnon and Achilles in the first book is a sophisticated
and fully observed presentation of verbal conflict between
real people before an audience. The fact that more than
forty per cent of the *Iliad* is speech, that the narrative
strategy, in Aristotle's words, is 'dramatic', and that in
Books 1 and 9 we have two major scenes of argument and persuasion may help us to understand something of what fifth-
century Athenians responded to in the Homeric poems.

We can go further. We are inclined to think that the
moment of realisation, the moment where human blindness and
the limitations of man's vision and understanding are suddenly confronted with undeniable truth in a lightning stroke,
always painful and often destructive, is another distinctive
mark of fifth-century consciousness and of the tragic
theatre in particular. 'At last I understand (ἄρτι μανθάνω)',
cries Euripides' Admetus (*Alc.*, 940); 'now I understand
(φρονῶ δή) the power that has destroyed me', says Hippolytus
(*Hipp.*, 1401) - 'now I am in my right mind (ἐγὼ δὲ νῦν
φρονῶ): I was not then', says Jason (*Med.*, 1329); 'all must
be out, all clear' cries Oedipus in Sophocles' play (*O.T.*,
1182) - 'the moment Cambyses heard the name of Smerdis, he
was struck with the truth of what Prexaspes had said, and
realised that his dream . . . had been fulfilled . . . . And
when he heard the name of the city, struck by the shock . . .
he came to his senses. The meaning of the oracle became
clear,' writes Herodotus (*Her.*, 3. 64) and others in his
history (Croesus is the prime example) come face to face
with a truth they have ignored. In all these cases, the language (μανθάνω, φρονῶ, σωφρονῶ etc.) is perhaps peculiar to
the fifth century, but the notion of a tragic realisation is
certainly not. The earliest, and in many ways the greatest
is Homer's: it is Achilles' realisation in *Iliad*, 18 (*Il.*,
18.72 ff.) that in being granted by Zeus the revenge upon
Agamemnon and the Greeks for which he had prayed, he has
lost the only thing that would have given that revenge sweet-
ness and meaning, the life of Patroclus. He was not there to
defend him when he encountered Hector, and for that Hector
too must pay the price and die - which will lead in turn to
his own death. He sees now at last that strife (ἔρις), 'that

is sweeter than the dripping of honey and swarms like smoke
in the hearts of men' has brought all this about, and he
wishes that 'it might vanish from among gods and men', but
too late. Indeed it is important to see that, for all the
straightforwardness and the moral simplicities of the
Odyssey's judgment on the actions of Orestes, there is a
tragic ambivalence in the morality of Achilles which makes
the story of his 'wrath' one of engrossing complexity:
Achilles' insistence upon the absolute nature of the obligation to defend honour and reject the smallest measure of
even a supposed humiliation constitutes the paradigmatic
case of a man who acknowledges the morality of contest and
honour, but that same insistence is what brings Achilles to
his tragic discovery of consequences he had not foreseen,
just as it brings Hector to his death. The germ of much
fifth-century tragedy is in it.

In other ways too we can see the fifth-century theatre
held in the grip of Homer's imagination. The Homeric epics
created an image of the Trojan war that exerted a controlling influence on the way that war is presented in fifth-
century tragedy. Even after the Persian wars had provided a
counter-image of conflict between Greeks and non-Greeks as a
struggle between civilisation and barbarism, between freedom
and slavery, the Trojan war remained essentially what it is
in Homeric epic: an image of human struggle in which the
heroism of Hector is not less than, nor different in kind
from, the heroism of Achilles, and in which the suffering
that war brings is embodied above all in the women of Troy,
in Hecabe and Andromache. The fact is quite remarkable, I
think, and worth underlining, and it is part of the lasting
legacy of the Homeric imagination. It means, for example,
that for the fifth century the Trojan war was simply not
available as an adequate image of the struggle between
Greeks and Persians (for that the sculptors of the Parthenon
metopes had to turn to the battles between Lapiths and cen-
taurs, between men and half-beasts, between gods and giants
and between Greeks and Amazons), and conversely that when a
fifth-century dramatist wants an image of the human suffering of war, all war, it is to the women of Troy that he
instinctively turns, as Euripides did in *Hecabe*, *Andromache*
and *Trojan Women*. Though it is not 'Homeric', it is none the
less a result of the impact on the fifth-century imagination
of the Homeric poems that Euripides can present the treatment of the Trojan captives by the Greek victors as itself
the act of 'barbarians': 'it is you Greeks,' says Andromache
in *Trojan Women*, 'who have devised barbarian cruelty'
(*Troades*, 764).

For my last example of the ways in which the Homeric poems

influenced the imaginations of the fifth-century dramatists,
I want to put forward a more speculative suggestion. The
chorus is clearly an expressive medium which has no direct
analogue in the Homeric poems, and whose origins lie in
quite other areas of Greek literary tradition. But the *way*
in which the dramatists make use of the expressive possibilities of the chorus may owe something, I suggest, to the
example of Homeric poetry. When Euripides, in *Medea*, has his
chorus of Corinthian women turn sharply away from contempla-
tion of Medea's ghastly design to avenge herself on Jason by
killing his (and her own) children (a design which they have
just explicitly and with gravity condemned in the name of
'the laws of men'), to thoughts of the perfect harmony in
climate and culture represented by Athens (*Med.*, 824 ff.),
the ironic commentary that this juxtaposition offers both on
Medea's plan, now cemented, to take sanctuary in Athens as
soon as she has brought off the infanticide, and perhaps
(for an Athenian audience in Athens witnessing a story en-
acted at Corinth) on the self-image of Athens, is unmistakeable. The technique of sharpening meaning by ironic juxtaposition is not peculiar to *Medea* (nor indeed to Euripides).
In *Electra* another chorus of women turns aside from an increasingly bitter and savage action of humiliation and
counter-humiliation and the obsessive desire for vengeance
to imagining the magnificent ships that long ago carried
Achilles almost joyously to Troy and then his armour,
brought to him by the nymphs, and culminating in a vision of
Achilles' shield: both scenes abound in glossy images, of
dolphins dancing to the sound of music and Perseus skimming
over the sea, carrying the Gorgon's head, without effort;
the sun's bright chariot and the dancing choruses of stars;
a helmet inlaid with gold and a sword with a worked blade
(*Electra*, 432 ff.). The jar between the romanticised language and imagery of this chorus and its context of brutal-
ity and bitterness is too palpable to be missed: we know
from its aftermath that the Trojan war was not like this. I
suggest that this technique of ironic juxtaposition is owed
to Homer, already used by him not with the sometimes savage
undertones of Euripides' juxtapositions, but with a broader
and gentler humanity. It is used already in the Iliadic
scene to which that Euripides chorus alludes, the shield of
Achilles in *Iliad*, 18, as Oliver Taplin has recently reminded us.[4] But it is used with more sophistication perhaps in
the *Odyssey*, both in Odysseus' tales and in the songs of the
bards on Ithaca and in Phaeacia. When Demodocus recalls,
first the quarrel between Odysseus and Achilles (*Od.*, 8. 73
ff) and then the entry of the wooden horse into Troy (*Od.*,
8. 499 ff.), he is singing after the feasting in Alcinous'

palace, to entertain the assembled Phaeacian βασιλῆες, and
to Odysseus himself. The Phaeacians are entertained: they
enjoy the songs as they are meant to, but Odysseus weeps:
these are tales but they are also Odysseus' experiences,
'the pains he suffered' of the opening of the poem. The
ironic confrontation of tale and experience, of hero and
audience comments both on itself, and on the world of the
Phaeacians. In between the two 'Iliadic' tales, Demodocus
has sung of the love of Ares and Aphrodite, an outdoor,
afternoon song to accompany a dance suggested by Alcinous as
a diversion from the tensions to which athletic competition
had given rise. It is a divertissement, enjoyed by all its
audience, Odysseus as well as the Phaeacian princes. A further ironic juxtaposition: the song of Ares and Aphrodite,
for the Phaeacians, is no less an entertainment, and no more,
than the songs of heroes at Troy, since both deal with re-
mote events in an imagined other world. But not for Odysseus:
the poetry of experience for one who has experienced it is a
different thing from an exercise of pleasant fantasy.

The poet of the *Odyssey* is acutely sensitive to the varieties of the tale, its shifting relationship to experience,
to singer or teller and to audience. In the first book,
Phemius sings to the suitors of the bitter homecoming of the
Greeks from Troy, and they sit in silence listening. But
Penelope comes down from her room, hearing the 'magical song
(θέσπιν ἀοιδήν)', and in tears asks Phemius to give over his
sad song and choose another, since 'you know many other
things to charm men with, the deeds of gods and mortals
which the singers make famous'. For her again Phemius' song
is no entertainment. But she is rebuked by Telemachus who
answers her with two arguments: it is not the singer who
causes the griefs that his song encompasses, but Zeus, and
it is the most recent song to which men give most regard
(*Od.*, 1. 325 ff.). The *Odyssey* is a tale full of the telling
of tales, and most of them make an oblique comment on the
world of the poem, and perhaps on the world of its audience.
Odysseus tells more tales than any other character in the
story and his tales are full of such ironic commentary. His
'lying tales', to Athena in Book 13, to Eumaeus in Book 14
and to Penelope in 19 are full of a masterly plausibility to
the utmost of *vraisemblance*, but we know with the superior
knowledge of the narrator of this whole tale that they are
false. By ironic contrast, the stories Odysseus tells to his
Phaeacian audience in Books 9-12 are fantastic, full of
strange creatures, spells, transformations and dream-like
action: they are incredible but they are true, and Odysseus'
audience in Phaeacia simply accepts them as true: 'they were
stricken to silence, held in thrall by the spell of the

story all through the shadowy halls'. (*Od.*, 11.333 ff. = 13. 1 ff.). 'Odysseus,' says Alcinous, 'you are no lying cheat. . . . The black earth produces many . . . who make up false stories from which a man could learn nothing. But there is a grace upon your words, and your mind is good. You told your story expertly, as a singer would do.' And we can smile at that, for what it says, obliquely, of Odysseus and the Phaeacians, of stories and story-telling, experience and art.

What I am suggesting is that, for the playwrights of the fifth century, there was everything to learn from the poetry of Homer. He was 'the poet', as perhaps only Shakespeare is for us, or as Dante was for Eliot, who had produced images of human experience that were true and right and timeless, in a variety of modes, and with a mastery and a sophistication that were, for Aeschylus, Sophocles and Euripides, their education.

NOTES

1. Cambridge, 1979.
2. *Sophocles: an Interpretation* (Cambridge, 1980) p.19.
3. Berkeley, 1968.
4. 'The Shield of Achilles within the *Iliad*', *Greece and Rome*, vol.xxvii (1980) no.1, pp.1-21.

4 Virgil's *Iliad*

K. W. GRANSDEN

The withdrawal of Achilles in wrath and pique from the
fighting, and the run of Trojan victories consequent upon
the successful plea of Thetis to Zeus on her son's behalf,
constitute the narrative core of the *Iliad*, Homer's 'wrath-
theme'. The structure of Virgil's 'Iliadic' *Aeneid* incorporates the Homeric motif of the hero's absence but it has been
transformed completely. In *Aeneid*, 9 Aeneas is absent from
the fighting which breaks out in that book because he is
away on a military mission. Virgil has assimilated the motif
of the hero's absence into a war story more Roman than
Homeric; the intense diplomatic activity of *Aeneid*, 7 and 8,
the opening of the Virgilian *Iliad*, is far removed from the
spirit and conduct of heroic conflict. Not only has Aeneas
sent Ilioneus to king Latinus and gone himself first to king
Evander at Pallanteum and then to king Tarchon in Etruria,
but the Italians, too, send an embassy to Greek hero Diomedes, now also settled in Italy: this embassy returns empty-
handed in Book 11, Diomedes having declined to re-engage his
ancient foe. All this activity Romanises Virgil's *Iliad* and
gives it a sense of exemplary historical purpose.

Book 9 starts with a transitional line linking the narrative to that of 8:

Atque ea diuersa penitus dum parte geruntur

(And while these things were happening far away) -

there then follow three successive spondaic lines charged
with a sense of foreboding:

Irim de caelo misit Saturnia Iuno
audacem ad Turnum. luco tum forte parentis
Pilumni Turnus sacrata ualle sedebat.

46

(Iris was sent from heaven by Juno Saturn's daughter
To Turnus the bold. By chance in the ancestral grove
Of Pilumnus in a holy valley Turnus took his ease.)

Turnus now takes the centre of the stage. The repetition of
his name, first in the accusative, then in the nominative,
is a characteristic Virgilian narrative device, the effect
of which is rather like the cinematic tracking of a camera
from one view-point to another; it is a way of controlling
and directing the reader's shaping of the narrative. The
sequence here is: Juno-Iris-Turnus. The line describing the
sending of Iris by Juno is repeated from 5.606, where it
inaugurates the episode in which the women of Troy, weary of
travel, set fire to the ships. Now in the ninth book another
attempt is made to burn the ships, this time by Turnus, an
attempt foiled by their miraculous transformation into
nymphs. The model of this miracle is the transformation of a
ship into a cliff of stone in *Odyssey*, 13. The elements of
the marvellous in the *Aeneid* are generally Odyssean (or
Apollonian) rather than Iliadic, even when they occur in the
'Iliadic' half of the poem. For although there are in the
Iliad some miracles and transformations, talking horses,
automatic robots made by Hephaestus, mists, plagues and
other visitations of the supernatural, nevertheless the
limits of the Iliadic world are more firmly bounded by
natural law than are those of the *Odyssey*, where things contrary to natural laws abound. The *Iliad* is strongly imbued
with a sense of human mortality, of man's powerlessness to
transcend natural bounds, of a general doom subject to
decrees which are seldom suspended. For the poet of the
Iliad, who could not allow Zeus to save his own son Sarpedon,
'not even the mighty Heracles escaped death' - that other
son of Zeus who in the *Odyssey* and in later myth, as the
Roman Hercules, became, like Aeneas, a deified hero. The
boundaries of the Odyssean world stretch beyond the fron-
tiers of death. Now at the start of his Iliadic narrative,
Virgil allows an Odyssean miracle to hold the reader a
little longer in an enchanted pastoral world where the laws
of probability do not operate.

What Virgil has done in the magical transformation of the
ships in *Aeneid*, 9 is to modify passages in the *Iliad* in
which Hector does actually succeed (after one foiled attempt)
in setting fire to the Greek ships, as part of the damage
inflicted on the Greeks during Achilles's absence. The
fighting in *Aeneid*, 9 goes the Rutulians' way in Aeneas's
absence, exactly as the fighting in *Iliad*, 8 to 16 goes the
Trojans' way during Achilles's absence. But an 'Odyssean'
miracle of transformation is assimilated to the grim Iliadic

narrative of battle, and offers a characteristically Virgilian symbolism. Just as the Shield in *Aeneid*, 8 was given a symbolic function over and above Aeneas's actual need of arms, so now, the poet asks the reader to observe that Aeneas no longer needs his ships. They have brought him home. Turnus, however, thinks the miracle is an omen in support of his cause. The Trojans, he cries exultantly, are now trapped. They must fight on land (and the dilemma of whether to fight on land or at sea recalls the dilemma of Actium), and on land I am unbeatable. They cannot escape. I do not need Vulcan to make me armour nor a thousand ships like the Greeks had to beat the Trojans, nor a wooden horse to hide in. I shall fight them in daylight and burn down their camp (9. 130-53).

The grandeur of this speech recalls many heroic orations of Ajax and Hector in the *Iliad*. It ends with the dismissal of his troops for supper and sleep, and this directs the implied reader to *Iliad*, 8 when Hector dismisses his troops after the abortive attempt to fire the Greek ships.

As we read on in *Aeneid*, 9, *Iliad*, 8 to 10 can be detected under the surface like the traces of an earlier text on a palimpsest. But these are not merely decorative or rhetorical allusions, but the start of a carefully constructed reworking of the entire central portion of the *Iliad*.

Night falls, on the Rutulian camp. Structurally and thematically, this is a re-enactment of the famous night-fall at the end of *Iliad*, 8. During this night, in the *Iliad*, two missions are undertaken: the unsuccessful embassy to Achilles by Odysseus, Ajax and Phoenix, which ends in his refusal to return to the fighting; and an intelligence reconnaissance, by Odysseus and Diomedes, during which they capture and kill the Greek spy Dolon and the Thracian king Rhesus and his chiefs and remove their horses. These two episodes, embassy or *presbeia*, and reconnaissance or *doloneia* take place in the same night and occupy the ninth and tenth books of the *Iliad*.

The famous ending of *Iliad*, 8 depicts the Trojans' nightwatch after their first successful day's fighting since Zeus began to fulfil his promise to Thetis, which had been in abeyance in Books 2 to 7 when the poet was performing various other introductory and recapitulatory episodes. After this nightwatch there is to be a run of Trojan victories, during the continued absence of Achilles, which will culminate in Book 16 in the death of Patroclus. Virgil has compressed the narrative structure of these books (*Iliad*, 8-16) into two books (*Aeneid*, 9 and 10). The nightwatch of the Rutuli in *Aeneid*, 9 also marks the start of a run of Latin victories which will culminate in the death of Pallas.

Virgil begins this sequence at 9.161. He incorporates a reminiscence of the start of *Iliad*, 9 when Homer shifts the
scene from the Trojan nightwatch to the camp of the Greeks,
who in their turn set guards while they debate their next
move. For in Homer, as we expect, the centre of the action
is not the temporarily victorious, ultimately doomed Trojans,
but the Greeks, temporarily on the defensive yet destined to
triumph, both in the war itself and more immediately in the
action of the *Iliad* after Achilles returns.

In *Iliad*, 9 and 10 Homer presents two Greek reactions to
the Trojan offensive. In *Aeneid*, 9 after a Rutulian night
scene corresponding to Homer's Trojan night scene at the end
of *Iliad*, 8:

> conlucent ignes, noctem custodia ducit
> insomnem ludo

> (The watch fires gleam, they while away
> The unsleeping night with dice -)

(9.166-7)

Virgil takes the implied reader back to *Iliad*, 9 to show us
Aeneas's men (as Homer had shown us Agamemnon's) wakeful
also: not confident and carefree like the Rutuli, not drinking and dicing but anxious at their leader's absence at a
moment of peril. For the war has begun in Italy.

The story of Nisus and Euryalus which forms the central
section of *Aeneid*, 9, although structurally modelled on
Iliad, 9 and 10, is wholly unhomeric in tone and treatment.
In Homer, the embassy and the *doloneia* are unrelated save
that both take place on the same night and both involve
Odysseus. The two episodes are themselves very dissimilar in
tone. The embassy is an affair of bitterness and heart-
searching, one of the finest, most reflective and important
episodes in the *Iliad*. Achilles not only rejects Agamemnon's
apology and refuses his gifts; he attacks the heroic code
itself. 'The coward and the brave man, they have both died
alike', he says, in the course of one of the most powerful
speeches in the entire *Iliad*, and his refusal to return to
the battlefield dominates the whole central section of the
epic. The *doloneia*, however, is on an altogether lower emotional plane. It takes no cognisance of the embassy just
ended; the situation is that which obtained at the end of
Iliad, 8. Agamemnon cannot sleep; worried about the Trojan
offensive he summons a nocturnal war-council, as a result of
which Odysseus (who has just returned from seeing Achilles,
though there is no reference to this) is despatched with
Diomedes to try to spy out the enemy's intentions. On the

Trojan side Hector makes a similar decision (a piece of
rather uninteresting epic 'doubling') and Dolon is despatched to try to find out if the Achaeans are still guarding
their ships or have decided on retreat. The events of the
doloneia are never again referred to in the poem and have no
apparent effect on the narrative of Book 11, where the
arming of Agamemnon formally signals the resumption of
hostilities.

Virgil's decision to combine the Homeric embassy and
doloneia into a single indispensable episode, the first conspicuous *aristeia* of his Iliadic narrative, is perhaps the
finest 'esemplastic' insight in the entire structure of the
Aeneid. Nisus and Euryalus, to begin with, are not spies but
rescuers, volunteers for a dangerous mission: to try to get
through the enemy lines to Aeneas, to inform him of the
impending danger and bring him back to the Trojan camp. They
fail, and die heroically. Their intense mutual affection,
which makes the passage so moving and so characteristic of
Virgil, has already been displayed in Book 5: they play a
prominent part in the footrace in the funeral games. An
accidental fall by Nisus, who slips on a puddle of blood,
offers a prefiguration of Book 9:

> Unlucky Nisus stumbles
> In some slippery blood, and already confident of victory
> Failed to keep his footing, overbalanced
> And fell down in the dirt and blood.

> (5.328-33)

Because of his love for his friend, Nisus, still on the
ground, trips the leading runner and thereby enables Euryalus to win the race. The foul is an interesting touch: we
are to regard the love of a comrade as an overriding emotion;
Virgil here establishes the lengths these two will go to,
the risk they are prepared to take, for each other's sake.

Nisus's love for Euryalus in 5 is reciprocated and mirror-
ed in 9, where the famous line

tantum infelicem nimium dilexit amicum

(Only he loved his unlucky friend too much)

> (9.430)

brings back the epithet first given to Nisus in 5. It also
recalls a passage in *Aeneid*, 1 crucial to the whole of
Virgil's *Iliad*, in which the poet first draws the reader's
attention to the tragedy of young men who die in wars - a
theme which dominates Virgil's epic in a way that it does

not dominate Homer's. Aeneas is in Carthage gazing on the
murals in the temple of Juno, where scenes from the Trojan
war are depicted, among them the death of Troilus (not, of
course, from Homer but from some later part of the Troy-
cycle):

> parte alia fugiens omissis Troilus armis
> infelix puer atque impar congressus Achilli.

> (In another scene there's Troilus running away,
> > weaponless,
> Unlucky boy, no match for Achilles.)

> > > > > (1.474-5)

Those lines introduce two important Virgilian motifs or
topoi: the death of young men, and the idea of unequal combat. They recur throughout the *Aeneid*. In 10, Pallas and
Lausus, both young, both doomed, are not destined to fight
each other, 'for each his destiny waits at the hand of a
greater foe' (10.438).

In Homer the motif of the tragedy of those who die young
is not developed. There is one very famous formular epitaph,
used of the deaths of both Patroclus and Hector, of whom it
is said

> The soul fluttering free of his limbs went down into
> > death's house,
> Mourning her destiny, leaving youth and manhood behind.
> > > (*Iliad*, 16.856-7 = 22.362-3)

But the idea of youth is not seen as specially poignant.
Homeric heroes are warriors in the prime of fighting manhood
(most of them have been fighting for nearly ten years) but
in Virgil's epic a clear and significant distinction is made
between chiefs like Aeneas, Turnus and Mezentius, and young
untried heroes like Pallas or Lausus, coming into battle
fresh like so many on the western front in the first world
war, protégés of the older and more experienced. (One tends
to forget that Patroclus, though less nobly born and a
lesser warrior than Achilles, was actually older). Virgil
finds deep pathos in the theme of the young soldier meeting
a superior foe; Homer does not. 'Patroclus too is dead, and
he was a better man than you', says Achilles fiercely to
Lycaon just before he kills him (*Iliad*, 21.107). 'Do you not
see what sort of man I am, how beautiful, how big, and I
come of a good father and a goddess mother, but on me too
death and strong destiny wait, some morning or evening or at
high noon.' For Homer, the overriding pathos is simply a

self-awareness of mortality, from which none in the *Iliad* is exempt.

Virgil chronicles not a few weeks in a ten year war but a complete war lasting a few weeks only. Death comes quickly to young men brought up to live in peace. Achilles's epic boast to Lycaon finds an odd echo in *Aeneid*, 10 when Aeneas kills Mezentius's son Lausus. He alludes both to Lausus's youthfulness and to his inadequate prowess:

> Do you go crashing in to your own death, taking risks
> you are too weak for?
>   (10.811)

Aeneas calls Lausus *infelix*, unlucky, (829, cf. Troilus and Nisus) and *miserande puer*, pitiful boy (825), and says it should console him that 'you die at the hand of great Aeneas' (830).

The phrase 'miserande puer' recalls another passage earlier in the *Aeneid* which throws light on the poet's deep sense of tragedy underlying the deaths of the untried. This passage is the description in Book 6 of Marcellus, Augustus's heir-designate, shown to Aeneas by Anchises in the pageant of heroes in the Elysian fields:

> Fate will let the world glimpse him for a little while
> only . . .
>   (6.869-70)

Marcellus too is called 'miserande puer': that he would have triumphed had he lived links his early death with the untimely deaths of Books 9 and 10. The story of Marcellus depends on the idea of rebirth, a doctrine which does not render the brevity of human life any less sad; indeed it perhaps renders it more so.

> stat sua cuique dies, breue et inreparabile tempus
> omnibus est uitae.

> (All of us have our day, brief and irrecoverable the time
> Of life for everyone.)
>   (10.467-8)

Those words are spoken by Jupiter to Hercules, in a significant context which is also relevant to our present concern. Pallas has just sent up a prayer to Hercules, who, as we learnt in 8, was his father Evander's guest at Pallanteum when he killed the monster Cacus. He has prayed to be allowed to kill Turnus. Hercules is powerless to grant such a prayer; it will take a greater warrior to kill Turnus. Jupiter then speaks the words just quoted, pregnant with Virgilian *weltschmertz*, and goes on to refer to his own son Sarpedon, who fell at Troy and he could do nothing, and whose death, moreover, in *Iliad*, 16 at the hands of Patroclus led to Patroclus's own death just as in *Aeneid*, 10 the death of Halaesus at the hands of Pallas leads to Pallas's own death, 'etiam sua fata uocant', for Turnus too destiny calls, says Jupiter (10.471-2). Throughout Virgil's *Iliad*, starting with the first *aristeia* and self-sacrifice of Nisus and Euryalus who, like the Romans on Aeneas's shield, *pro libertate ruebant*, fell for freedom, the sense of *déjà vu*, already established in the Elysian fields, is overwhelming. For every rebirth there must be yet another death.

The story of Nisus and Euryalus is highly dramatic. The two friends are on watch, the fires burn through the night; Nisus speaks, and his opening words are striking in their impatience, as though he can no longer contain himself:

> Do the gods instil in us, Euryalus, this buring desire
>   /   for glory,
> Or is this dreadful longing the god inside us all?
>   (9.184-5)

This dreadful longing, *dira cupido*, has already figured in *Aeneid*, 6 in that same context of reincarnation to which we have just referred. Aeneas asked the Sibyl 'whence comes this dreadful longing for life?' (6.721). The hero who has suffered so much cannot understand how anyone who has reached the larger air and ampler light of Elysium should wish to be reborn, yet the life-force recurs and fights the regressive death-wish. Nisus's outburst is also relevant to the entire *Aeneid* and is a comment on the heroic code of Homer's *Iliad* as set forth in Sarpedon's speech to Glaucus in *Iliad*, 12.310-28. Do our passions come from outside us (Ate, the disturber of men's reason, referred to by Agamemnon in his quarrel with Achilles) or from within? The question had been tackled by Lucretius but for Virgil no scientific theory can satisfy a profound uncertainty, a sense of the unanswerable. The question falls like a shadow across the whole poem, from its very first lines - do heavenly beings really feel such wrath? asked the poet about Juno - to its last book and the poet's last question about war, 'was this your will, O Jupiter?'

Nisus's speech shows the same love for Euryalus which he displayed in the foot race. Again, it is of his friend not of himself that he thinks.

You can see how sure of things the Rutulians are:
Hardly a light shines over there, relaxed with drink and
                                                          sleep
They've gone to bed. All's quiet. Now listen.
I've been thinking, and this is my plan.
Aeneas must be got back - all of us are saying it,
Somebody's got to go and tell him what's happening.
If they promise to give you what I shall ask them - as for
                                                           me,
The deed itself is glory enough - I think I can find
A way through the lines by the foot of that hill to
                                        Pallanteum.
                                                (9.188-96)

The Latin is simple and straightforward, the tone direct.
But Euryalus insists on going too, and his words seem to
pick up the concept of 'dira cupido': for this love of glory
is death-bound:

   est hic, est animus lucis contemptor et istum
   qui uita bene credat emi, quo tendis, honorem.

   (Here's courage holds cheap the light and thinks that
   Glory you go to worth the price of life.)
                                        (9.205-6)

'Here's courage holds cheap the light': this contempt for
life is a profoundly Virgilian emotion; it is not found in
the *Iliad*. In the speech of Sarpedon to Glaucus, for instance, it is made clear that risks have to be taken because
men are mortal: if they were not, there would be no incentive, no point, in taking the risks; yet the risks are certainly not taken to court death, nor is there any inherent
virtue in taking them. For Virgil, despite his access to
spiritual consolations unknown to Homer, fate and death con-
spire to produce a sense of life as in itself tragic, something to be endured rather than enjoyed, with none of
Homer's exuberant vitality and zest.
   The narrative of *Aeneid*, 9 is written in a direct and
simple style which is yet quite unhomeric. Virgil had
evolved for his early *Eclogues* a style of charming if
studied simplicity. In his maturity he seems to have revived
that style, but now it is deeper, plainer, less self-
conscious, the pathos and sentiment stronger. At the very
start of his *Iliad* he seems to have wanted to involve the
reader's pity and love.
   The actual tale, too, is more immediate and dramatic than
Homer's *doloneia*. At Homer's war-council the volunteers are

already present when the mission is discussed. In Virgil's
narrative, the Trojans ponder how to get news of their vulnerable situation to Aeneas; Nisus and Euryalus burst into
the tent, their plan ready, and put it across with all the
enthusiasm and force of youth. The incentive is with them.
The structure of the scene is fully integrated into the
Iliadic *Aeneid*, of which it is a paradigm, determining the
whole tone and treatment of the war-narrative which forms
the poem's last four books. Virgil has shed the element of
traditional randomness which links the *doloneia* so loosely
to the monumental *Iliad*.

In Homer, the embassy is essential to the wrath-theme, the
doloneia is not. The *doloneia* for what it is worth, is a
success, the embassy a failure, since Achilles does not and
cannot return until provided with a proper psychological incentive in Patroclus's death. Yet it is not the *doloneia* we
want to read now, but the embassy, the failure of a mission,
with its long resonant speeches, its psychological insights.
The story of Nisus and Euryalus is also a failure, but not
of bitterness and rejection. Virgil's own involvement is
deeply felt and fully declared:

> Fortunate pair! if my poem has any influence,
> No day shall ever take you from time's memory,
> So long as Aeneas's house by the immovable rock of the
>   Capitol
> Shall stand and the fathers of Rome have dominion.
>   (9.446-9)

In the *Aeneid* the prophetic future occurs frequently in the
first eight books but virtually disappears from the Iliadic
narrative of 9 to 11, to return in the final scene between
Jupiter and Juno in 12 which balances the opening scene
between Jupiter and Venus in 1 where the doctrine of
'imperium sine fine' is set forth. In 9 to 11 there are only
a few brief excursions into the future, and these are of a
special kind, for they are undertaken by the author himself,
not the narrator of the new *Iliad*, largely realised in the
historic present, but the implied author, the commentator,
directing the implied Augustan reader towards a construction
of the poem's meaning which the modern reader must now take
as part of the poem's pastness. The Capitol has fallen, yet
the *Aeneid* still has power to move the modern reader through
the *aristeia* of Nisus and Euryalus. The fact that *aristeia*
has outlived the imperium changes the poem for the modern
reader.

In the *Iliad* Helen says of herself and Paris

we two, on whom Zeus set a vile destiny, so that hereafter
we shall be made into song for men of the future.
(Iliad, 6.357-8)

This is a clear reference to that tradition of heroic song
of which the monumental <i>Iliad</i> is itself the culmination.
Helen's words are guaranteed by the fact that they appear in
precisely that song for men of the future to which they look
forward. But there is no instance in Homer of the poet himself claiming to preserve an event by his song, and this is
surely evidence of that oral tradition on which his song
depends. The motif of the artist's power of immortalising
events became a <i>topos</i> in post Homeric literature, from
Pindar to Horace and on into the Renaissance. Virgil continued to pay lip service to the remembering Muses but now they
are his servants as they were also Milton's:

Vos, O Calliope, precor, aspirate canenti
quas ibi tum ferro strages, quae funera Turnus
ediderit, quem quisque uirum demiserit orco,
et mecum ingentis oras euoluite belli.

(You, O Calliope, I pray, inspire your singer
To know what deaths and destructions at this time Turnus
Dealt forth, what heroes each man sent to the underworld,
And with me unroll the mighty documentary of war.)
(9.525-8)

The emphasis has changed from the song on the lips of men,
to the singer: canenti ('mihi' understood), 'mea' carmina.
Virgil uses the mode of direct address not only in the epitaph for Nisus and Euryalus, but again at the death of
Lausus:

Here death's cruel accident and your most glorious deeds -
If the antique past shall be credited with such works -
Yes, and yourself shall be my song . . .
(10.791-3)

There is a more complex and significant instance earlier in
10, when Pallas is killed:

Ignorant is man's mind of destiny and the future,
And can't control itself when fortune boosts it.
For Turnus the time shall come when he'll pray for Pallas
To be unharmed, give anything for that, loathe
This day, these spoils . . .
O you who return to your father, source of much sorrow and
pride,

This was your first day of war, your last also.

(501-8)

Here, after a generalising comment on human blindness to the
future and human hubris, Virgil addresses Turnus in his
moment of exultation, echoing the warnings of the dying
Patroclus to Hector and the dying Hector to Achilles. Then
Virgil addresses the dead Pallas, intensifying further the
emotional involvement the reader already shares with the
author. Homer too had employed the mode of direct address to
a hero, most remarkably in 16 when he addresses Patroclus as
his death approaches:

So in your fury you pounced, Patroclus . . .

(16.754)

There, Patroclus, the end of your life was shown forth . .

(16.787)

And now dying you answered him, o rider Patroclus . . .

(16.843)

The effect of these addresses is to abolish for a moment the
narrator, the traditional and impersonal bard, to create a
bond of empathy between the singer and the song. The poet
becomes author, a figure not only controlling his narrative
but also involved in it, intensely aware (as the hearer can
only gradually become) of having reached a moment in which
feeling is too strong to be left to speak wholly for itself
inside the characters and their story. Our sense of grief
for Patroclus is not wholly conveyed through the grief of
Achilles, though his words and actions from the beginning of
Iliad, 18 to the end of the poem constitute the principle
directing force of the feelings the hearer must experience.

Thus Virgil increases this 'vatic empathy', though he does
not originate it. Our sense of grief for the fallen young
heroes in the Virgilian *Iliad* is not wholly subsumed in the
grief of those (chiefly Aeneas himself) who mourn them; the
author himself insists on an intense and deliberate controlling empathy - not just the emotional pressure which might
be generated by a crucial passage in the narrative, as
Patroclus's death prompted Homer to a bold use of the voca-
tive, but an empathy so pervasive and sustained that the
reader may find himself constructing out of an epic of heroic action another epic of a very different kind, an epic of
sensibility and *weltschmertz* only partly derived from the
grief of Aeneas, fully motivated as it is in the narrative,
the reaction of an Augustan Roman at the horror of *discordia*,
a kind of proleptic shudder of memory.

The episode of Nisus and Euryalus forms the centrepiece of
Book 9, which, like so many books of the *Aeneid*, has a tri-
adic structure. The long final section, describing the
assault on the Trojan camp, marks the first full-scale narrative of general fighting in the Virgilian *Iliad*. It is
written in the poet's grandest style. It is not only - and
here it continues the technique of the episode just ended -
a re-enactment of the *Iliad*, it is also a continuation of it.
History repeats itself, but there is also development and
extension. Early in the passage, when the Volsci, allies of
Turnus led by the warrior maid Camilla, mount the first
attack on the camp, the Trojans find themselves once more in
a situation with which they are all too familiar:

adsueti longo muros defendere bello

(9.511)

They are 'well used to defending their walls in a long war'.
The spondaic line, as so often in the *Aeneid*, slows down the
reader (the reader using translations may not be sensitive
to this effect) until he feels the static weight of perpetual defensive campaigning pressing on the unlucky Trojans;
behind the verse is the whole of the *Iliad*, and with the
Homeric legend something else - the Augustan sense of Rome
having passed through what seemed like almost perpetual
defence against Etruscans, Gauls, Carthaginians, and against
the enemy within herself.

The attack culminates in a striking passage in which Turnus is actually shut up inside the gates by Pandarus, perhaps
an allusion to the wooden horse in which the Trojans had
fatally shut their foes inside their gates. This time, however, the siege will be relieved, the defenders will be
victorious. Another mighty spondaic line marks Pandarus's
effort to shut the gates:

portam ui multa conuerso cardine torquet . . .

With mighty force he turns the gate on its hinge
Using his shoulders, leaves many of his own army
Outside the walls, unprotected against the struggle,
But others he shuts in with him as they rush headlong.
Fool, for he did not see that charging in their midst was
                                              king Turnus,
And he actually shut him inside with them,
Like shutting a tiger in with cattle.

(9.724-30)

Book 9 begins the *aristeia* of Turnus. The model for this is

the *aristeia* of Hector in the Trojan breakthrough in *Iliad*,
12. But the relation between Aeneas and Turnus and their
Homeric archetypes Achilles and Hector is a complex one.
Turnus plays both roles; so does Aeneas. The fluctuation of
the Homeric roles is an important element in the structure
of Virgil's *Iliad*. And there is a good reason for it. For
this is a war which nobody loses. After the defeat of Turnus
the two sides, Latins and Trojans, indigenous and immigrant,
will become one nation. Thus the Homeric concepts of victory
and defeat are in a sense irrelevant in the *Aeneid*, or they
are transcended. As a Trojan, Aeneas avenges the death of
Hector and is a second Hector, but this time a victorious
one. Turnus is, in the words of the Sibyl's prophecy to
Aeneas in *Aeneid*, 6, a second Achilles born in Latium await-
ing a second Troy: but this time, if he is Achilles he will
die, as indeed did Homer's Achilles, whose self-awareness
that by staying in Troy he is doomed (he often threatens to
go home but cannot resist playing out his hand against fate)
adds much to the tragic power of the *Iliad*.

In Book 9, the absent Aeneas is playing the role of the
absent Achilles which in Iliadic terms works in with
Turnus's replaying of the role of Hector on the offensive.
Yet when Turnus finds himself inside the enemy walls he
naturally recasts himself as Achilles, for the Trojans are
now on the defensive as the Greeks were temporarily during
Hector's *aristeia*. When Pandarus taunts him

This is not the stronghold of your native Ardea;
You are in the enemy camp and you can't get out

(9.738-9)

his reply is obvious:

You'll be able to tell Priam that you found here another
Achilles.

(9.742)

But Turnus's triumph, like that of Hector in the *Iliad*, is
short lived. As Achilles returned, so will Aeneas.

We must never forget that the Trojans have just escaped
from the most famous military defeat in the ancient world.
Their role as challengers in Latium (for so they have now
unwillingly become) must have seemed to the indigenous
leaders fairly incredible and naturally elicits various un-
flattering sneers at their military record, most notably in
the taunts of Turnus's brother-in-law Numanus in the last
section of Book 9. He refers sneeringly to the Trojans'
defeat at the hands of the Achaeans, and asks them if they

are not ashamed to face a second disaster, not this time at
the hands of the Greeks but of a much tougher people,
'patiens operum paruoque adsueta iuuentus' (607), young,
used to hard work and roughing it. If the Trojans could be
beaten by the Greeks, who in Augustan times were not
regarded as a race of warriors, how can they have the nerve
to take on the Italians? All this is addressed to the
implied Augustan reader. Virgil's account of the tough
('duri') Italians in Numanus's speech carries the same moral
implications as the famous portrait of the hardworking
Italian farmer in his second *Georgic*; there is the same contrast between simplicity and effeminate luxury. Just as the
farmer is the antitype of the city dweller with his fine
house and dependence on foreign luxuries, so the Italian is
the antitype of the Trojan, effeminate in dress, oriental in
origin, devoted to the worship of strange gods and goddesses,
especially the Magna Mater (Great Mother): it is a deliberate irony of the poet's that earlier in 9 we have seen the
women of Latinus's city, under the influence of Juno-Allecto,
behave in the uncontrolled and orgiastic fashion now attri-
buted to the Trojans, who are first called Phryges (a people
despised by the Augustans for their effeminacy) and then
Phrygiae, Phrygian women. So in the *Iliad* Thersites sneered
at the Achaeans as women, and Priam after Hector's death
referred with contempt to his other sons as heroes of the
dance floor. Paris's preference for love-making over fighting is also mentioned in the *Iliad* several times, notably in
3, and the metamorphosis of Aeneas himself into a second
Paris, ready to take another man's wife, is another element
in the manipulation of figures in the poem. Aeneas must move
through the roles of Paris (discredited) and Hector (defeat-
ed), and finally reassume the role of Achilles, dispossess-
ing Turnus of that claim.

So Turnus will see the role of Achilles slip from his
grasp when victory seemed certain. What defeats him is
finally Aeneas, but before that, his 'caedis insana cupido',
his crazy lust for slaughter. The madness of war, symbolised
earlier in 7 by the visitations of Allecto, sweeps over the
victorious hero; instead of concentrating on strategy, he
behaves like an old-fashioned Homeric hero obsessed with
self-displaying prowess. He kills many Trojans, but in Roman
eyes this *aristeia* is magnificent but it is not war. The
reader will think continually of the ten-year siege of Troy,
ended not by any *aristeia*, but a ruse, an intelligent stra-
tegem.

Virgil modifies the *Iliad* in many ways, not the least important of which is that he passes judgment, through the
Aeneid, on its attitudes to warfare. The Trojans in Italy

put to good use the lessons of Troy. The Rutuli just made
the same mistakes as the old heroes, failing to follow
through advantages, obsessed with personal glory. If only,
says Virgil, Turnus had simply opened the gates and let his
army in, that day would have been the end of the war - and
of a nation. But he did not. When in Book 10 Aeneas kills
Mezentius, this is not mere *aristeia*: he is the most dangerous enemy leader after Turnus and must be eliminated; when
Camilla is slain only Turnus stands between Aeneas and victory. But Turnus makes no comparable killing in 9. Instead,
he wears out his strength in strategically valueless
slaughter. Mnestheus rallies the Trojans at the end of the
book. His words carry a grim warning: if they lose this
siege too, where next can they find refuge, what other walls
can they hide behind? The appeal coincides with a divine
intervention: as with Achilles in *Iliad*, 21, a victory for
Turnus now would be 'beyond what is fated'. The strength in
battle which Turnus is losing as the day wears on is now
taken from him by Juno; the hero's powers flag; he retreats,
plunges into the Tiber and is carried back to his comrades.
This leap into the Tiber is a 'pre-echo' of Horatius Cocles'
famous leap: Cocles is depicted in Aeneas's Shield, along
with Cloelia, an Etruscan hostage who also escaped into the
Tiber and swam to safety.

Turnus's retreat is itself an Iliadic turn in the fortunes
of war. In *Iliad*, 8 the unfinished battle book, in which the
Trojans first succeed in counterattacking during Achilles's
absence - the start of Zeus's fulfilment of his promise to
Thetis - Hector nearly breaks through despite the opposition
of Hera; but night falls, too soon for the Trojans, welcome
to the Achaeans. The surge of fighting in 8 is ineffectual
and confused, the real break-through for Hector not coming
until later. The triumph of Turnus in 9 is the triumph of
Hector, first the unsatisfactory and interrupted attack in
8, then the resumed and greater *aristeia* of 15 and 16. In 15
the exhortation of Nestor to the Achaeans to acquit themselves like men is the model for Mnestheus's exhortation in
Aeneid, 9. In the *Aeneid*, the Rutulian attack in the Trojan
camp is interrupted, as Hector's attack is frustrated in the
eighth book of the *Iliad*, by the divine intervention of Iris.
Turnus, exhausted by personal vendetta, retreats at the
moment of potential triumph (another Homeric echo, Ajax
under fire in *Iliad*, 16). In the ebb and flow of attack and
counter-attack which articulate the enormous narrative of
the *Iliad*, the unfinished battle book of *Iliad*, 8 offers a
check to the Trojan offensive which surges forward again
through the central books of the poem. Virgil has a much
shorter narrative span for his *Iliad*, four books, into which

he compresses the broad outline of the Homeric conflict from
Books 8 to 22; but his structure of movement and counter-
movement is sharper, less wayward, tighter and pays scrupulous attention to the laws of cause and effect and to military probability. He does not try, nor would he have been
able, to represent the multiplicity of views, voices, characters, perspectives, the sheer density of Homer, a poet
working with an enormous mass of traditional material in
which the emphases continually shift within and around the
narrative core, never quite lost sight of for long, the
choice or perhaps the invention of Homer himself, the story
of the wrath of Achilles.

The endings and beginnings of books in a 'carmen perpetuum'
(continuous poem) are of special significance. They expect,
and bear, close scrutiny. They carry the reader across gaps,
allowing him either to pause in his reading or to continue.
They articulate changes in time and place. They pick up
echoes, anticipate or confirm parallels and correspondences,
bring into the mind images and symbols from an earlier point
in the narrative or from a later point recalled from earlier
readings. The river Tiber is a very important symbol in the
Aeneid. It is the Simois and Xanthus of the Italian *Iliad*,
in the prophetic words of the Sibyl 'multo spumantem
sanguine', teaming with much blood (its fellow river is the
Numicus, where Aeneas's death and translation occurred). It
is the way by which Aeneas reaches the site of Rome. It
forms the pastoral transition of the opening passage of
Virgil's *Iliad*. It dominates the first section of 8, in
which Aeneas prays for protection to the personified and
manifest Tiberinus:

> O father Tiber with your sacred stream,
> Receive Aeneas and keep him safe from peril at the last.
>   (8.72-3)

Now at the end of 9 it receives Turnus, washes his wounds,
bears him back safe to his comrades. The word *laetum* is
strikingly and perhaps strangely applied to Turnus in the
last line of 9; it was a key word for the receptive, eager
and optimistic Aeneas of Book 8. But Virgil needs to emphasise that the river of Italy receives and succours all her
sons, indigenous no less than immigrant. Structurally, the
end of 9 takes us back to the pastoral opening of 7 and com-
pletes the third quarter of the epic and the first half of
the Iliadic 'maius opus'. It makes a beautiful and histori-
cally significant reference to the river as a source of suc-
cour. It offers a decrescendo in the narrative leading us
briefly away from the war and preparing us, by a strikingly

dramatic transition, to read the opening of 10, the council
of the Olympian gods, which grandly ushers in the last movement of the poem.

Thus in *Aeneid*, 9 Virgil has begun his *Iliad*, his 'maius
opus', and also the task of writing the Homeric wrath theme
out of his *Iliad*. But in writing out the wrath theme he did
not write out wrath. There is much wrath in the last books
of the *Aeneid*, and Aeneas himself does not escape it, but it
is the wrath of Achilles against Hector, not against Agamemnon. When in *Aeneid*, 9 Aeneas returns to the fight he returns in triumph at the head of fresh Etruscan troops. Now
Homer's Achilles also returned to the fighting in *Iliad*, 20
at the head of his Myrmidons. But he returned after and
because of Patroclus's death. Aeneas returns from an absence
prompted not by wrath and pique and refusal to fight (un-
thinkable in a hero renowned alike for 'pietas' and military
prowess) but by military necessity. He has been behaving not
like a sulking Homeric hero but like a Roman 'dux'. And he
returns to the war before the death of Pallas. Indeed he
cannot prevent that death; it lies heavy on his heart
throughout the sombre eleventh book. Pallas had been entrusted to his protection. But he did not cause his death, as
Achilles's wrath had let Patroclus die. Virgil had to write
the wrath theme out of his *Iliad*, for the enormous and para-
noid egotism of Achilles was inappropriate to a Stoic hero
and father-figure of the nation.

5 The Epic Theme of Love

JOHN BAYLEY

Among the many spacious classical compositions, now coming
back into fashion, which were executed by Lord Leighton
during the late Victorian period, is one of that favourite
subject of heroic art, the rescue of Andromeda by Perseus, a
rescue that was of course the prelude to one of the comparatively few stable and, one assumes, happy unions recorded in
Greek legend. Leighton's treatment of it is sufficiently
striking, his canvas being dominated by the sea-serpent,
whose dark bulk forms a cave in which Andromeda seems, even
if shrinkingly, to have installed herself. In this situation
the assailant threatening her might even be Perseus himself;
she seems at any rate withdrawn into a kind of provisional
domesticity, regardless of all the strenuous goings-on about
her. Some fifty years earlier, Ingres had painted his celebrated picture with a similar subject, the rescue of
Angelica by Ruggiero, taken from Ariosto's epic, *Orlando
Furioso*. Here too we may be struck by the element of dis-
paration that dominates the form. Clad in a complete suit of
Cinquecento armour that would have delighted Viollet-le-Duc
or Sir Walter Scott, and which indeed had been copied by
Ingres from funerary hatchments in Rome, Roger is far too
preoccupied with his great spear to pay any attention to the
wilting Angelica. Her own pose might as equally be suited to
romantic reverie in a Rousseauesque landscape, or beside the
urn of the young Werther, as it more obviously is to a
sexual tableau arranged by the Marquis de Sade. Emphatically
she is not a domestic figure; and we may recall that her
subsequent adventures in the epic indicate a very different
sort of girl from the Andromeda wedded to her deliverer
Perseus.

Incongruous elements are never wanting to the epic. It was
a strength of the form that from the time of the Greeks it
contained the anti-epic, the mock-heroic, as naturally and
with as many possibilities of further enterprise and evolu-
tion, as the novel has proved to contain the anti-novel. But

these two pictorial examples suggest that there may none the
less be a difference between the kinds of isolation and
instability we associate with nineteenth-century romanticism,
and the sorts of incongruity which the epic form and style
has always taken in its stride. The epic assumes a social
relation between gods and men, as between men and monsters;
and this stands for a corresponding relation between the
highest and the lowest parts of man's nature. It is this
predictable and harmonious relationship which is so conspicuously missing in the nineteenth-century treatment of a
heroic theme. The proprieties of the accepted and the incongruous have there - in those two pictures - flown off into
anarchy, into a host of unrelated impressions. There are in
them no correspondence of high and low parts, but only elements subjective and discrete, responded to in the isolation
of the musing and surveying consciousness.

But when treated by a Titian, or by a Rubens, the pictorial elements in the heroic theme of love and rescue flow as
easily together as do the various aspects of the composition.
In the Prado, Rubens Andromeda welcomes her rescuer with a
smile as charming as it is suitably 'bien élevée'; at once
natural and spontaneous and also the proper response of a
princess in difficulties to Perseus's gaze of chivalric,
ardour: meanwhile a gambolling Cupid extends towards the
pair the already lighted torch of love. The situation is not
wholly serious, but when were the time-honoured tales of
heroic mythology ever wholly serious, in the sense in which
the word is used today? The 'seriousness' of our artists,
whether novelist or painter, is always self-conscious. It
cannot escape the imputation of earnestness, the fatal imputation which has clung, however undeservedly in his case, to
Matthew Arnold's phrase for the effect achieved by lofty art
- 'high seriousness'. What, one might ask, is low seriousness? Arnold's phrase inevitably misleads, because it seeks
to misuse for a special purpose the serenity and inclusive-
ness of epic; it cannot help implying solemnity, and vigil-
ance in the maintenance of solemnity.

The epic is never earnest, because its events retain in
narration the paradox of what actually occurs, of what
occurs simultaneously to man as a spirit and man as an animal, an object in space. This is the most natural kind of
incongruity, and is suited to the survey in the epic manner
of all human transaction, not least to the invention of
amorous encounters, and to the portrayal of heroic as well
as domestic and conjugal love. Tolstoy, with his profound
admiration for Greek literature, understood this very well.
The epic quality in *War and Peace* is unmistakable and was
intended to be so. More striking in terms of the theme of

love is the way in which both the tradition of epic and the
tradition of Greek tragedy are made simultaneous use of in
Anna Karenina. The story of Anna's love for Vronsky is
tragic; it is a visitation from which she cannot recover and
which in the end destroys them both. Like tragedy it all
seems arranged beforehand, but Tolstoy succeeds in dissipa-
ting that impression by the way in which he naturalises the
fatal love in all sorts of details and observations, domestic and psychological; and by placing the love tragedy
beside an epic account of courtship and marriage, a combination that succeeds in making us feel that the whole truth
about both stories is being told.

That phrase - 'the whole truth' - is of course used by
Aldous Huxley in this context. In his essay 'Tragedy and the
Whole Truth' he observes that Homer, unlike any artist in
the genre of tragedy, could not help telling 'the whole
truth' about life. The main example he gives is from the
Odyssey, when the survivors of the encounter with Scylla and
Charybdis cook a supper to stay their hunger before giving
themselves up to grief for their dead comrades. Huxley's
attitude approximates rather self-consciously towards a
tough, no-nonsense one of 'that's all the facts when you
come to brass tacks'. He implies, as many other writers
would do today, that eating is essential, grief a luxury and
a pretence. This attitude subtly falsifies the narration of
Homer, for Huxley's view of the matter is reductive where
Homer's is not. The 'truth' of Homer's account depends on
the impartiality of the balance, on its assumption that all
things have their rightful place. All man's needs are equally needful to him: his body and soul have an equal part in
all his doings.

Nor is Huxley on very sure ground, in my view, in his
implication that such a wholly truthful epic narrative is
something archaic, almost primordial, something naive, that
disappears after the Homeric age. I think in fact that the
mode by which narrative establishes this impression of truth-
fulness is probably common to all good epic, whatever degree
of artificiality, of latterday imitation and sophistication,
may be involved. In any such epic the same premises - the
premise of incongruity necessary and taken for granted -
still hold. The high style, the accepted language of the
lofty spirit, continues to recognise and dignify the activities of the body. That style, in the context of epic, is
suited to the relation of any human activity. Knowing this
as they did, or at least conditioned to it as they were, the
neo-classic poets of the eighteenth century found it natural
to make the effect over-ornate and over-explicit, to ham it
up by deliberately describing trivial or mundane activities

in epic terms. But the harmonious relation of high and low
is no more mocked by the mock-heroic than is the idea in
poetry of the heroic itself; each depends on the other, and
is strengthened and confirmed by the other's existence in
poetry.

It is a part of the confirmation that both wear a social
aspect. To be high, or low, activity or emotion cannot be
solitary and subjective. The wholly social aspect of love,
as of grief, is shown by Virgil's Hecuba, calling her husband and children together in the last extremity, when the
Greeks have broken into Troy.

> "huc tandem concede; haec ara tuebitur omnis,
> aut moriere simul". sic ora effata recepit
> ad sese et sacra longaevum in sede locavit.
>
> (*Aeneid*, 2.523-5)

Drawing the old man to her, and placing him on the sacred
seat, makes him a child again, as if that social and natural
bond gave some earnest of preservation. Religion and the
family, twin necessities of earthly existence, come and
cling together in the threatened imminence of death. Love
itself is not a talent, an accomplishment or a revelation,
but a mere requirement of survival.

It is true that Virgil has a more difficult time than
Homer, his great predecessor, in the matter of narrative
contrivance, the art all story-tellers must grapple with of
getting in what has to be got in as naturally and plausibly
as possible. It is here that C.S. Lewis's term, 'secondary
epic', may be a useful way of making a distinction, for a
post-Homeric narrative is usually tied to some metaphysical
requirement or project, which serves in its turn to give the
narration the weight or epic status. In 'secondary epic'
nothing is glossed over or left out, but a certain conspicuous artfulness may be needed to explain why things took
place as they did. Thus, when Aeneas evacuates Troy, plot
requires that his wife Creusa should follow a little distance behind the party of husband, aged father and small son.
In this way she can become separated and disappear, exactly
what took place remaining 'incertum', her fate unknown. Such
a fate would itself draw attention to the cohesiveness of
the family, more emphatically but in the same way as does
the passing reference in the *Iliad* to Helen's brothers and
her enquiry after them, ignorant that they are long dead and
buried back home. But what would today be called the coding
of his operation requires Virgil both to eliminate Creusa
and to explain the fact with all propriety. Aeneas still has
to encounter Dido, and to win the Latin Princess. In conse-

quence, what should have the calmness of fate acquires something of the bustle of contrivance. Virgil's lack of freedom
means that his hero has to protest a little too much. Aeneas
rushes back to find his wife: he even risks calling out for
her by name in the streets thronged with Greek enemies and
pillagers. He is let off the hook, not for the last time in
his pilgrimage, by Creusa's ghost, prophesying his auspici-
ous future and bidding him search for her no more.

   Dido is less forgiving than his amiable wife, but the
Roman connexion determines his nature in that context too.
To turn again to our pictorial analogy, a Renaissance version of the parting of Dido and Aeneas, even one by a manner-
ist such as Manetti, maximises the Virgilian loftiness of
the conflict between love and duty, one-sided as it is,
while at the same time managing to show how special interest,
or plain prudence, lurks in the background of all high and
passionate human transaction. The eighteenth century well
knew how to formalise the feeling in a witty antithesis. 'I
sighed as a lover, I obeyed as a son' Gibbon tells us in his
autobiography. He is not being consciously Virgilian about
his love affair in Switzerland, but there is no doubt that
the tradition of Aeneas is in the background, and no doubt,
too, that Gibbon intends us to take the point that love for
him was as real as was the filial piety and prudence. Pope
had created the same effect in the poetic antitheses of his
mock-epic, *The Rape of the Lock*.

   Whether the nymph shall break Diana's law
   Or some frail china jar receive a flaw;
   Or stain her honour, or her new brocade,
   Forget her prayers, or miss a masquerade.

Honour and a dress are both important matters: if both parts
of the antithesis were not equally relevant it would fail of
its effect. A modern Huxley-type assumption, that girls in
practice think only of their dresses and not of their honour,
trivialises the issue and the art involved. Of course the
tradition has become infused with a conscious satire, but
the assumptions of the heroic situation are none the less
preserved. Generations of schoolboys have been laboriously
informed that the 'piety' displayed by Aeneas, however prig-
gish it might appear in a modern setting, would have been
wholly admired and taken for granted in the culture of the
time. But is that adjustment really necessary? is it not
even positively misleading? It might be wiser to infer that
a Roman reader of the Augustan period would very well understand and take for granted the situation and its issues, the
character of the hero and its significance, for the private

life and for the founding of a state. And an audience conditioned to the relation of high and low takes it for granted
that the first, in the style and context of epic, can include the second, but not vice-versa.

It is true that Virgil has to work hard to arrange matters
- that is part of the challenge of this style of epic - and
Milton consciously took up the even more taxing task of ren-
dering in epic terms the paradoxes of creation and the fall
of man. But on his side was the fact that incongruity is
built into the epic and heroic plan, accepted as a part of
the human and divine specification. Adam and Eve act the
part of the epic audience attentive to

> things so high and strange, things to their thought
> So unimaginable as hate in Heaven,
> And war so near the peace of God in bliss.
>   (*Paradise Lost*, 7.53-5)

Unimaginable in that context maybe; but in practice all the
more imaginable because so familiar from the epic and human
context. Milton is the great conjurer of the form, exploiting to the full not only all its devices but all its implications in the field of war and peace, love and enmity. But
before turning to him it is worth remarking on the more
imponderable ways in which Chaucer and Shakespeare adapt the
epic world of incongruity, the high and the low, and especially in relation to the theme of love. Chaucer narrates the
history of Troilus and Cressida in a manner calculated to
bring out to the full the absurdity and the heroism, the
tenderness and the calculation in it. The low and the high
were never brought into more effective juxtaposition, as
they are in the most elaborate and ambitious of the Canter-
bury series, the *Knight's Tale*. It has recently been argued
that this most knowingly harmonious of Chaucer's master-
pieces is in fact a straight satire on the gap between the
ideal of knighthood and its practical application in the
field of mercenary warfare, a claim that ignores the proven-
ance of the artistic method and its acceptance of the way
things are and have always been. Chaucer's interpretation of
his methods and materials, from Virgil to Boccaccio, is
always in the direction of further insight and delicacy, a
bringing out of contrasts taken for granted in his various
sources, such as that between the public persona of his
heroine Emily, a persona dedicated to 'love' in the official
sense, and her diffident and incoherent private being.

That incoherence is more marked in the Shakespearean handling. Antony and Cleopatra are fully aware of their heroic
status as lovers, but they are quite unable to disguise from

the audience or from each other the confusion and vulnerab-
ility which in the end brings them more surely together than
the lofty sense of roles and fates. But both states are a
part of them, and in art each depends upon the other, the
godhead of the Queen of Egypt and the sense of her as 'no
more but e'en a woman'. The deliberate disbalance in *Troilus
and Cressida* has the effect of making audience and characters alike seem to crave, even if they hardly know it, for
the heroic ideal of love and honour which contingency and
expedience destroy in the act at every point. But Shakespeare's most remarkable dramatisation of heroic love and
its opposite is in *Othello*, where tragedy and tragic outcome
depend precisely on the inability of the lofty style and the
love ideal to withstand the envy and derision of the low
view, or to compromise with the sexual nature of the human
animal, the fact that, as Iago says of Desdemona, 'the wine
she drinks is made of grapes'. In *Othello* the epic need for
the incongruous, and the harmonies that attend it, are
graphically shown by a war between the low the the high -
Iago and Othello - which results in their mutual destruction.

In terms of style the collusion between low and high
becomes a matter of secrecy, of what is both revealed and
concealed - the one by means of the other. Where the understanding of much great verse is concerned that tacit understanding is itself a kind of pleasure principle. It would be
hard to exaggerate what a radical change took place when
incongruity disappeared as an accepted feature of poetic
style, to be replaced by a verse structure which directly
imitates the feeling and narration it expresses. Such a
structure, however it may manifest itself, is the distinguishing feature of 'modernism', which has been around now
for quite a while. The old incongruity is manifested in
Wordsworth's instinctive adoption of a diction of heroic
propriety to recount in the *Prelude* his interior experiences
and the movements of his mind. Leopardi's wordless afflic-
tions, comforts, timidities, and ennuis find the same kind
of voice, a very different voice from the modern tones of
Robert Lowell or John Berryman, whose poetry depends for its
overwhelming authenticity on seeming not to be poetry but
the utterance of one exactly in the state described. But
Wordsworth's or Leopardi's state of mind assumes that its
natural concomitant is the lofty and euphonious clarity bestowed by an art habituated over many centuries to dealing
with anything experienced by humanity: and dealing with it
by setting up a counter-style to the inevitable shapeless-
ness and incoherence of that experience.

That style dies hard, surprisingly hard, in spite of all
that modernism can do. And the secret source of vitality is

the way in which what is variously and traditionally incongruous can continue not only to please but to surprise. Many
of Hardy's finest poems are rich in the epic incongruities,
and although Hardy could not be called a poet of modernism
he is in no sense old-fashioned either but wholly 'sui
generis'. Eliot, too, can use a version of the high and low
styles, as he does in the *Quartets* and particularly in the
second part of 'East Coker', the one acting as statement and
the other as commentary on it. In a rather similar way an
epic eloquence in pentameters is used with an effect almost
of parody by Wallace Stevens, when the argument, that poetry
can no longer transform and elevate the bare nature of
things, itself becomes the reason for an elevated diction.
  A famous sonnet by the early twentieth-century American
poet, Edward Arlington Robinson, provides an engaging example
of the way in which the incongruities that always lurk in
epic metaphor can take on fresh life and establish in a new
context the majestic eroticism of the high style. The sonnet
is in the pastoral vein, a description of harvest. The octet
moves with calm Tennysonian confidence over the ripening
corn - 'green wheat was yielding to the change assigned' -
and over an unspoken meaning in the pace and tempo of
natural process. Then the sestet weaves its way towards a
burst of anthropomorphism.

> So in a land where all days are not fair,
> Fair days went on until another day
> A thousand golden sheaves were lying there
> Shining and still, but not for long to stay -
> As if a thousand girls with golden hair
> Might rise from where they slept and go away.

The image startles by its very conventionality, and by both
multiplying and simplifying the epic image of dawn rising
from the bed of Tithonus. As often with such successfully
manipulated metaphor we have a simultaneous recording of the
magical with the literal, the poetically marvellous with the
comedy of actual fact. A thousand sleeping girls getting up
together and walking off is an extravagantly comic idea that
succeeds by liberating the lurking homeliness in such an
image as that of dawn rising from her lover's couch; and yet
managing at the same time to seem inevitable and decorous, a
predictable movement in the poetic diction. The effect is of
a stage further - almost surrealist - extension of the per-
sonification in Keat's *Ode to Autumn*, Autumn herself, or
himself, encountered 'on a half reaped furrow sound asleep',
with the simple weariness of an ordinary mortal at harvest's
end. In both cases a conventional grandeur of fancy contrives

to coincide with a simplicity of fact, as they do too in
such a Renaissance picture as the Rubens I spoke of.

There is the further echo in that sestet of an epic movement of words from Milton, the one in *Comus* when the atten-
dant spirit in guise of a shepherd describes the sovereign
herb that will undo enchantment, and which is compared to
'that Moly/That Hermes once to wise Ulysses gave'.

> The leaf was darkish, and had prickles on it,
> But in another country, as he said,
> Bore a bright golden flower, but not in this soil:
> Unknown and like esteemed, and the dull swain
> Treads on it daily with his clouted shoon;

'But not in this soil - but not for long to stay.' It is a
very characteristic Miltonic movement and once again asserts
the coincidence of the marvellous with the everyday, and of
both with what is passing. That formula comes to its perfec-
tion in the story of Adam and Eve in *Paradise Lost*. Our
general parents, their destiny and their love, are a prime
instance of the exploitation of epic incongruity. They are
made in the image of God, and in their naked majesty dwell
like gods in the garden of Eden. But they are also human,
and will fall through the commonest of human failings, curiosity, vanity, disobedience. Yet it is these failings, too,
which will make them heroes, god-like again in the fidelity
and love they show each other after the fall.

With the fearlessness one would expect, Milton introduces
the incongruous elements, the god-like and the human, the
spiritual and the physical, in every context of his epic.
Critics - C.S. Lewis was one - have suggested that he makes
a successful distinction, not in any case too difficult to
arrange, between fallen and unfallen sexual love. The reality is perhaps rather more complex, and more satisfying.
Milton is explicit at every stage of their relation, and at
every stage appropriately mingles suggestions of the low and
the high. Take the moment in Book 4 when Adam and Eve walk
hand in hand to their nuptial bower and prepare to retire
for the night.

> This said unanimous, and other rites
> Observing none but adoration pure,
> Which God likes best, into their inmost bower
> Handed they went; and, eased the putting off
> These troublesome disguises which we wear,
> Straight side by side were laid; nor turn'd, I ween,
> Adam from his fair spouse, nor Eve the rites
> Mysterious of connubial love refused: (4.736-43)

Literal account then modulates into invocation, and thence
to disquisition.

> Hail, wedded Love, mysterious law, true source
> Of human offspring, sole propriety
> In Paradise of all things common else!
> By thee adulterous lust was driven from men
> Among the bestial herds to range;

(4.750-4)

The word 'mysterious', twice repeated, conveys the nature of
the sacred, the altars and the flame; but conveys it in a
way that also suggests the everyday nature of the sacred in
an epic context, the rites that are part of daily routine.
The domestic institution of marriage is part of the divine
order of Eden, the only private and personal relation in an
otherwise undifferentiated Paradise; and, more than that,
its rites contain a mystery which is not shared by ordinary
procreation. Naturally enough we do not learn what this is.
The point is referred to in a gamesome manner by Sir John
Suckling in his 'Ballad on a Wedding'.

> What that is, who can tell?
> But I believe it is no more
> Than thou and I have done before
>   With Bridget and with Nell.

In the language of poetry, and of epic poetry, Milton has
successfully established the idea that marriage is a privi-
leged state, belonging to the God-like part of men, but also
hallowing in a highly satisfactory manner every instinct of
their quotidian lower being.
The same interchange of high and low penetrates the masterly psychological analysis of the lovers after the Fall. Two
states result. One is of primitive cunning and calculation,
appropriate to the jungle law of a desecrated Eden. But the
other is truly heroic, only to be attained by man at a
crisis of his fate, and at his best and highest. No attempt
is made to explain the paradox, which is achieved by a brilliant use of epic dispassion and the epic style. Having
tasted the fruit Eve's reaction is exultant, but competitive:
the war between men and women has broken out, as the earlier
war did in heaven. She may have escaped the attention of
'Our great Forbidder, safe with all his spies/About him'.
But how about the problem of Adam?

> But to Adam in what sort
> Shall I appear? Shall I to him make known

As yet my change, and give him to partake
Full happiness with me, or rather not,
But keep the odds of knowledge in my power
Without copartner? so to add what wants
In female sex, the more to draw his love,
And render me more equal, and perhaps,
A thing not undesirable, sometimes,
Superior, for inferior, who is free?

(9.816-25)

'This way and that dividing the swift mind' Eve's mental
activities have all the solidity of epic, but also a fresh
agility conferred by her position as one divided between the
majesty of new creation and the enactment of an age-old kind
of mental intrigue worthy of Iago himself.

This may be well: but what if God have seen,
And death ensue? then I shall be no more,
And Adam, wedded to another Eve,
Shall live with her enjoying, I extinct;
A death to think! Confirm'd then I resolve,
Adam shall share with me in bliss or woe:
So dear I love him, that with him all deaths
I could endure, without him live no life.

(9.826-33)

Eve's train of thought is not ultimately ignoble; it has the
logic of possession about it. I must survive because I love
Adam, and because I love him he must be the same as me. This
idea succeeds and modifies the idea of emulation and rivalry,
and is as authentic if equivocal an expression of love in
its context as is her speech after God has passed sentence
upon them. Then she genuinely desires that the sentence
shall fall on her alone.

                    Both have sinn'd; but thou
Against God only; I against God and thee
And to the place of judgement will return,
There with my cries importune Heaven, that all
The sentence, from thy head removed, may light
On me, sole cause to thee of all this woe,
Me, me only, just object of his ire.

(10.930-6)

Adam reveals similarly incongruent emotions, now heroic and
fitted to the noble actor in a tragic scene of love trium-
phant in adversity, now as proper to the lowly scene of con-
nubial discord.

>   . . . with thee
> Certain my resolution is to die:
> How can I live without thee, how forgo
> Thy sweet converse and love so dearly join'd
> To live again in these wild woods forlorn?
> Should God create another Eve, and I
> Another rib afford, yet loss of thee
> Would never from my heart: no, no! I feel
> The link of nature draw me: flesh of flesh,
> Bone of my bone thou art, and from thy state
> Mine never shall be parted, bliss or woe.
>
>   (9.906-16)

This moving resolve is in keeping with Milton's presentation
of love, like the Creation and the Fall themselves, in terms
of free will. Adam could have disociated himself from his
guilty wife. But of his own choice he elects to be destroyed
with her, if destruction is to be their part. This indeed is
a 'glorious trial of exceeding love'. And it is worth notic-
ing how Milton manages to make Adam's decision seem unexpected, even surprising; for although the Fall was as much
foreseen by God as the founding of Rome was foreordained,
the decision to join Eve in destruction none the less seems
Adam's own, and made on the spur of the moment. Aeneas, of
course, could make no comparable decision in regard to Dido,
but then Aeneas's 'love' for Dido is something that has to
be subordinated to a higher duty. Adam gives the impression
that though his higher obedience to God forbids it, he makes
in his love for Eve a freer and nobler choice.

But this moving resolve does not prevent him from taking
it out on Eve in an all too husbandly manner. It does not
prevent his cry of 'Out of my sight, thou serpent!' when Eve
seeks his forgiveness, nor their mutual bickering after the
eating of the forbidden fruit, when Eve produces the most
exasperating of all wifely arguments.

> Being as I am, why didst not thou, the head,
> Command me absolutely not to go,
> Going into such danger, as thou saidst?
>
>   (9.1155-7)

Book 9 closes in this 'mutual accusation', in which neither
is 'self-condemning'.

> And of their vain discourse appeared no end.

A sufficiently realistic presentation of the trials of the
married state, as Milton had no doubt experienced them, and

as Homer himself had shown them existing between Zeus,
father of gods and men, and his wife Hera. But in Milton
this presentation coexists with something vital to the
spiritual and intellectual theme of love. Eve's argument is
not only on the true note of married discord; its unfairness
reveals the main and lofty theme of the epic, in matters of
love no less than in those of religion and worship. God has
established freedom in his own creation: he has made the
pair free to stand or fall, and Adam has rightly conferred
the same freedom in love on his wife. He was right to let
her leave him that morning, to encounter on her own the serpent and the fatal apple. For Milton love and worship are
alike matters of free choice, not bound by laws, as in the
Roman church, or by any absolute fiats of God and man.
Choice is vital in love as in religion, and free choice is
the link between human love and God's love for his creation.

The really significant factor, then, is Milton's instinctive use of incongruity, underlying and taken for granted by
the epic form and endorsed by his own wonderfully idiosyn-
cratic style and art. Interplay of the low and high elements
- heroism and calculation, majesty and meanness - create in
the relations of Adam and Eve an effect of the whole truth.
And this is where the epic's presentation of what in its art
is always true of human beings - bodies and spirits, gods
and animals - is more important than the specifically Miltonic picture of fallen and unfallen sex. Human psychology is
as accurately revealed before the Fall as after it. The
'sweet austere composure' with which unfallen Eve greets
Adam's objections to her going gardening on her own, is a
reaction with which any post-lapsarian husband would be familiar, at any time and place.

In their unfallen state our general mother and father
engage in sex as in a mystery. Nakedness means mysterious-
ness - 'Nor those mysterious parts here then conceal'd'. It
is a typical Miltonic paradox. Milton contrives to make
fallen and unfallen sex correspond to its two functions in
classical epic, where it can be a part of religious ritual,
a sacral mystery, as when a mortal girl is possessed by a
god, or a piece of normal quotidian business, private rather
than mysterious. But if sex in Milton corresponds rather
ingeniously to its functions in the epic, he has also both
borrowed and transformed what the epic implies about the
nature of love, making it much more moving, or rather more
movingly explicit. Adam and Eve are almost by accident, as
it seems, a touching portrait of mutual tenderness and dependence in a situation which becomes as precarious and uncertain, after their expulsion from the Garden of Eden, as life
was for the inhabitants of a heroic age, where death or

slavery waited at any moment, if fate so decreed. Adam himself pronounces that acceptance of things as they happen
which is the philosophy of such an age.

> But past who can recall, or done undo?
> Not God omnipotent, nor Fate.
>
> (9.926-7)

And he speaks the words at the moment of his own greatest
heroism - the decision to share death or punishment with Eve
- a moment which in its 'glorious trial of exceeding love',
as Eve calls it, is ethically quite unlike any comparable
moment in classical epic, and yet emotionally refers us back
to such moments. Eve herself echoes in words of touching
dignity and simplicity that recognition of impending fate,
and its consequent picture of mutual love as a clinging together in the face of circumstance.

> While yet we live, scarce one short hour perhaps,
> Between us two let there be peace.
>
> (10.923-4)

That peace of intimacy in a terrible world is as needful
between Adam and Eve as it is between Hector and Andromache.
And it has as little to do with tragedy as with romance. The
romantic love of an Othello is like the epic struggle and
reward itself, like the 'pride, pomp and circumstance of
glorious war': Othello wins his bride like a battle, as an
epic hero might triumph in single combat. Indeed it might be
said that the romance takes the military side of epic - confrontation, rivalry, the exercise of the will - and applies
it to the field of love. The consequences are often tragic
because two incompatible things, love and the will, have got
mixed up. Othello and Desdemona do not quarrel, as Adam and
Eve do; they confront each other in an affection which is as
great as its ignorance. It is a fatal passion, though Shakespeare's skill makes us feel that it is not necessarily tragic, that given time the lovers would have come to know and
need each other as much as they are now as romantically in
love with each other. Love passion in epic, like that of
Phaedra or Dido, is usually a disastrous thing, the frenzy
induced by a god. And the frenzied jealousy of Othello leads
to tragedy as does the passion of a Phaedra or a Dido. But
as there is no tragedy in the death of Hector and the be-
reavement of Andromache, so there is none in the fall and
condemnation of Adam and Eve. As handled by Milton, the
Fortunate Fall fits perfectly into the epic framework of
what is ordained, the 'moira' which foredoomed Troy, and

which neither gods nor men can prevent.

Later writers, even in a different genre, if they have an instinctive understanding of the incongruities of epic, can create comparable kinds of effect. Tolstoy, most analytical of novelists, can sometimes produce such a thing as if it were self-evident, when he is describing the emotion of love in relation to the customs and expectations of a patriarchal order. This contrasts, of course, with the tragic theme - the self-absorbed passion of Anna and Vronsky. One of the most moving moments in *Anna Karenina* is Levin's sudden exaltation, before his wedding, at the thought that Kitty loves him. This love has not declared itself in any passionate or emotional way, but is manifested to him in her deep and visible relief that she has found a good husband and will not be an old maid. That unexpected blending of the personal with the impersonal is very typical of the epic world. For Levin, the realisation that he is not, as it were, loved for himself alone is profoundly reassuring and gratifying. He is playing his part, like a denizen of epic, in the general picture and the eternal scheme of things.

At the other end of the great period of the novel, in its first English beginnings, Chaucer has the same instinctive understanding of epic effect, and the ability of a conscious craftsman to manipulate and make use not only of its characteristic decoration and decorum but also of its calm and simple incongruities. Sometimes, indeed, they become material for what seems and probably is a conscious joke, though Chaucer's jokes often avail themselves of the inscrutable dignities of the epic form. After the dramas of the *Knight's Tale*, and the foreordained death of the hero Arcite in the moment of his victory, a traditional kind of family comfort is taken and bestowed - an effective office of love.

> No man mighte gladen Theseus,
> Savynge his olde fader Egeus,
> That knew this worlde's transmutacioun,
> As he had seyn it chaungen up and doun,
> Joye after wo, and wo after gladnesse:
> And shewed hem ensamples and lyknesse.
>   'Right as ther deyed never man', quod he,
> 'That he ne livede in erthe in som degree,
> Right so there livede never man', he seyde,
> In al this world, that som tyme he ne deyde.
> This world nis but a thurghfare ful of wo,
> And we ben pilgrimes, passynge to and fro;
> Deeth is the end of every worldly sore'.
> And over al this yet saeyde he muchel more
> To this effect . . .

So might the father of King Cepheus have bestowed comfort if
his grand-daughter Andromeda had indeed been taken by the
monster. 'Joye after wo, and wo after gladnesse' is the attitude of the epic, both to the events it describes and the
emotional relationships it implies. Chaucer is only giving
his own note of fond and inspired parody to the normal note
of epic proposition, bringing out the fact that senile dis-
guisition can be both moving and tedious, comforting and
absurd. The tears of things, the solace of legendary precedent, are no less moving and less weighty here because they
are being proffered by an exceedingly boring old party. The
incongruity is recognised and drawn out by Chaucer in order
to make it more of a feature of style than it ever was in
the stately climax and anti-climax of true epic. Chaucer is
half way towards the deliberate exploitation of incongruity
that has now become a virtual convention of the novel, but
which in the epic lay under the calm surface. The novel of
course analyses love, and makes of its contradictions a feature of the analysis, but the epic takes it for granted, as
it takes for granted everything else in the human situation,
not so unlike the church in Philip Larkin's poem,

In whose blent air all our compulsions meet,
Are recognised, and robed as destinies.

6 Homer in Byzantine Dress

TOM WINNIFRITH

The study of Byzantine history can never replace the study
of the Classics. With a Thucydidean or Polybian view of history it is useful to gain some knowledge of a world which
with its desperate array of long term problems and short
term solutions may seem more relevant today than the Pelopon-
nesian or Punic wars. As Eastern Europe becomes more important to us it is useful to know something of Byzantium,
since most Slav nations owe almost nothing to the Roman
Empire and almost everything to the Byzantine Empire. It is
useful if we travel as tourists to Greece, and so many of us
do, to know something of the period between Alexander the
Great and Zorba the Greek, and yet how few of us do. The
achievements of the Byzantines in architecture and painting
are at least as impressive and a great deal better preserved
than the monuments of Classical antiquity. But the reason
why a study of the Classics has and must continue to have
pre-eminence for Western man and all mankind lies in its
literature. Here the record of Byzantium is far less impressive. A few hymns, the lives of saints, some romances, a
number of historians, imitating the style but hardly living
up to the standard of Thucydides, and innumerable tracts
full of stale theological subtleties represent a poor
achievement for a thousand years of history. It might be
argued that the West did not do much better, but then it did
not have any access to Greek literature, nor was it so
materially prosperous, as the rough crusaders discovered
when in amazement they entered the luxury of Constantinople.
Byzantine copyists by preserving Classical manuscripts for
posterity have ensured that we are in their debt, but by
trying to preserve the language of the Classics, while the
spoken language moved forwards, have ensured that the interest on this debt and the interest in the preservers is not
very heavy. In the West political and religious unrest led

to the satire and allegory of such writers as Dante, Chaucer
and the author of *La Roman de la Rose*; in the East, as
Professor Mango has so well explained in *Byzantium* (London
1980), a touching confidence that Constantinople was the
centre of the world, that the Emperor was God's elect, that
Greek was the language in which God had given his revelation
to the world, that this revelation, unchanged and unchanging,
could not be improved upon or extended, but only edited and
interpreted, hardly led to intellectual enquiry or literary
originality.

Byzantine civilisation does have its literary monuments,
and chief among them is the epic of Digenis Akrites, almost
unknown in the West, but known and appreciated by all sec-
tions of the community in Greece. As a folk hero Digenis is
a conspicuous figure in numerous popular Greek songs. The
villagers of the Pontus expected him to rise up, armed with
his mighty club, against the Turks in 1923. Colonel Grivas
in his campaign against the British in Cyprus took the code
name of Digenis. As well as these living survivals of the
Digenis legend we have a literary epic. A version of this
epic, 3182 lines long, divided into ten books was discovered
at Trebizond in 1875, and published in 1875, but the manuscript of this version is now lost. In 1878 another version
was found in Andros, 4778 lines long, and also divided into
ten books. In 1879 in the Greek monastery of Grottaferrata
near Rome a third manuscript of 3709 lines, divided into
eight books, was found. This is the earliest manuscript,
probably dating back to the fourteenth century, and is the
basis for the most accessible English edition, that of Mavrogordato. In 1880 a rhymed version of 3094 lines was published; this manuscript is in Lincoln College, Oxford. In 1904,
a manuscript of only 1807 lines was found in the Escorial
Palace near Madrid; this version, published in 1910, is very
confused. There is a prose manuscript at Salonica University,
and a Russian version was assembled in 1972 from three
eighteenth century manuscripts. Finally there are the akritic songs of the Greeks in Asia Minor with Digenis or a
character like him as hero. Anyone with even moderate
Ancient or Modern Greek can read any of the originals except
the last two without much difficulty. There is a literal
translation in Mavrogordato's edition and also an American
translation with the accurate but not very happy title *The
Two Blood Border Lord*. Both translations are based primarily
on the Grottaferrata version.[1]

The different manuscripts are not like the manuscripts of
classical texts, which miss the odd line or two or alter the
odd word. They are really different versions of the same
story, although some are closer to each other than others,

and it is possible, though difficult, to postulate an
elaborate stemma of how one version relates to another. Most
scholars assume an eleventh century proto-Digeneid written
or orally composed at about the same time or shortly after
the events of the poem, and assume the variations of the
different versions to be either the fault of oral composers
improving the original or of literary redactors trying to
improve upon the original, or of a combination of these
factors.

All versions deal with the dark but heroic days of the
Byzantine Empire between 800 and 1100, when its Eastern
boundary, roughly parallel to the Eastern boundary of modern
Turkey was defended by ἀκρίται, semi-independent warlords
charged with looking after the frontier. Of such warlords
Digenis was a supreme example, rightly admired by the
Emperor who appears in the poem to praise him. Oddly the
story begins not with Digenis, but with his father, an Arab
emir, who falls in love with a Greek maiden and carries her
off, but is eventually reconciled to his in-laws by being
conveniently converted to Christianity. Hence the name
Digenis, meaning 'of two races', although the Emir himself
would seem to have some Greek blood in his veins. Digenis
grows up and slays the odd bear and lion. Like his father he
falls in love with a lady, carries her off and is reconciled
to his in-laws who throw a magnificent party. In the central
section of the epic Digenis relates some of his exploits to
a Cappodocian. These exploits include a defence of his
wife's virtue against dragons and human enemies, and a
slightly less successful defence of his own virtue against
various temptresses. He builds a mighty palace, then his
mother dies, then he himself dies, predeceased by his wife
who dies out of love for him.

Much of the work on *Digenis* has either been historical,
tracking down references in the poem to historical person-
ages and events, or has involved literary history, tracing
sources of, parallels with, and derivations from the poem,
or has focussed on a study of the poem's language, comparing
one version of the poem with another, comparing the written
versions with the Akritic songs, and trying to decide when
and how the poem originated and was composed. Little work
has been done in trying to decide what kind of poem *Digenis
Akrites* is, and whether it is a good poem or bad one, and on
this basic question there is singularly little help from
those who have conducted detailed investigations into the
history, literary history and language of the poem, or
indeed from those who have given more general accounts of
the poem.

The historical, literary and linguistic research that has

been lavished upon *Digenis* cannot be entirely ignored, although those interested in the poem as a work of art cannot
have much in common with those who look upon it as a source-
book of information about Byzantine history in the ninth,
tenth and eleventh centuries. Much of this historical scholarship appears to be misdirected. The exploits recounted in
Digenis cannot be dated with any precision. When the Emir,
Digenis's father, is politely addressed by his future
brothers-in-law they express the hope that he may visit the
mosque at Palermo.[2] Palermo was in Arab hands from 831 to
1072, and these two dates are convenient termini within
which the events described seem to be taking place, although
at times there may be a harking back to earlier traditions.
At times, as when the Emir's uncle is said to have led his
army to Smyrna by the sea[3] we seem to be dealing with the
critical period of Byzantine history in the eighth century
before the Macedonian dynasty when there were Arab raids as
far as Constantinople. At times when Digenis lives in peace
by the Euphrates we seem to be talking about the eleventh
century when the Arabs were a spent force and Byzantium was
stronger than ever before. Although the poem is entitled
Digenis the Borderer it is odd that we never know exactly
where the border is; it seems to ebb and flow between Cappo-
docia in the middle of Turkey and Mesopotamia in the East in
the same way that the frontier itself fluctuated during the
course of the Macedonian dynasty. Three emperors are mentioned in the various versions of the poem, called Basil,
Romanos and Nikephoros. Nikephoros, not mentioned in the
Grottaferrata version, is presumably Nikephoros II (963-9)
rather than Nikephoros I (802-11), but Basil, who confusing-
ly in the fourth book of the Grottaferrata version both
exiles Digenis's grandfather and meets Digenis himself,
could be either Basil I, the founder of the Macedonian dynasty (807-86) or Basil II, the Bulgarslayer (967-1025).
Other versions of *Digenis* substitute Romanos for Basil;
Romanos Lekapenos (920-44) is the most likely candidate here,
but we could have a reference to Romanos II (959-63) or even
at a pinch the eleventh century Romanos III (1028-34) or
Romanos IV (1068-71).[4] The last two might seem rather improbable epic heroes, but there are plenty of precedents for
turning real life geese into epic swans.
     Given these basic difficulties about time and place exact
historical information becomes hard if not impossible to
extract. Of course most historical approaches to
accept that there are many different historical strands
woven into the poem. In trying to argue for instance that
Digenis's grandfather Chrysoherpes was Chrysocheir, the Paul-
ician heretic killed in 872, or that Aaron Doukas, one name

for Digenis's maternal grandfather, was a Bulgarian who died
in 1070[5] historians are not worried by inconsistencies within the poem, which clearly went through many revisions, of
which the many versions are both a symptom and an additional
complication.

But in admitting that *Digenis* is a poem with many layers
of history embedded in it, the historians appear to be putting *Digenis* in a category with other poems, not normally
associated with historical truth. The most obvious of such
poems are the *Iliad* and the *Odyssey*, and because we do not
have any history apart from the uncertain evidence of archae-
ology with which we may compare the events and way of life
associated with the Homeric poems, these poems are usually
but wrongly regarded as historical. So too are the South
Slav epics celebrating the resistance of the Serbs to the
Turkish conquest, although here we do have evidence which
contradicts the poetic account. Vuk Brancovic, the traitor
in the Kosovo ballads, was not necessarily so treacherous as
he appears in the poems. Marko Kraljevic, who appears in
literature as a Digenis-like figure, slaughtering Turks left,
right and centre with his club, seems in history to have
fought at Kosovo on the Turkish side.[6] If we want a more
modern example of how even recent history can be distorted
by primitive heroic poets there is a poem collected by
Milman Parry in which all the Balkan wars and treaties of
the nineteenth century are confused.[7] Perhaps the best parallel with *Digenis*, because it was written at the same time
and about the same type of hero, is the *Chanson de Roland*;
behind this account of a mighty battle between Christians
and Muslims, full of unhistorical details like the Christians getting as far south as Cordoba in the time of Charle-
magne, lies an obscure battle against the Basques.[8]

The reason why it is important to establish that *Digenis*
is not historical is not just that historical researches
distract us from examining the poem's literary worth. By
making the poem a historical one we diminish its literary
worth. As Cervantes saw in *Don Quixote*, historical truth and
epic poetry do not go together; when in the eighteenth century English poets tried to write long epics on historical
subjects, these were a dismal failure.[9] *The Chronicle of the
Morea* is not very reliable as history, but its historical
nature is one of the factors preventing it from being an
epic poem. It is true that in Book IV of *Digenis* the poet
when comparing the exploits of his hero with those of classical antiquity dismisses the latter contemptuously as myths,
but this is a commonplace of epic poetry: we find almost
exactly the same stance taken by Milton.[10] Nor of course
must we by emphasising the remoteness of *Digenis* from

historical truth conclude that the poem must therefore be a
romance. The boundary between epic and romance is less easy
than the division between fact and fiction.

Like Homer and the Serbian epics *Digenis* seems to be a
poem in which various levels of historical fact are incorpor-
ated and at the same time adapted into fiction for poetic
reasons. Putting *Digenis* into this class has obvious dangers.
It does not come out very well in comparison with Homer or
the Serbian epics, being less well organised than the former,
less simply and nobly heroic than the latter. Moreover,
though thanks to the researches of Lord and Milman Parry we
know a good deal about the oral composition of South Slav
heroic poetry, and as a result of these researches we think
we know a good deal about the oral composition of Homer with
its features, so similar to Serbian poetry, of repeated
passages, repeated lines and repeated formulae, we simply
cannot make the same inferences about *Digenis*. For, though
all versions of *Digenis* have the omissions, duplications and
confusions, characteristic of oral poetry, though the different versions of the epic, and the presence of akritic
songs would seem to suggest oral composition, there remains
the indisputable fact that *Digenis* does not contain the
repeated formulaic phrases which since the time of Milman
Parry we have come to associate with oral poetry.

In trying to decide whether *Digenis* is a literary or an
oral poem, we have to consider the problems of relating one
version of the poem to another, and of course the relation
of all the written versions to the indisputably oral akritic
songs. Mavrogordato says that the world of the akritic songs
is a completely different one from the world of the literary
epic, being full of magic. Even in the literary poem the way
in which Digenis conquers his enemies is hardly realistic,
but Mavrogordato is certainly right in saying that the akritic songs are so far removed in content from the written
versions of the poem that we cannot look to them for much
help about its composition. *Digenis* may have been woven together from rude lays, but the akritic songs are not the
rude lays in question.

The written narratives have apart from the Russian version
enough in common for us to be able to postulate a common
ancestor for them, a proto-Digeneid. Work done by Morgan
suggests that the muddles and confusions in the Escorial
version are a result of confused oral transmission at a fairly late stage.[11] In all versions literary allusions and a
monastic flavour in certain passages suggest a series of
monkish reviewers, altering usually for the worse the original poem. Mavrogordato takes the view that the Grottaferrata
version is not very different from the proto-Digeneid,

although the murder of Maximo after she has seduced Digenis,
which only occurs in this version, seems a sorry piece of
monastic revision. Morgan thinks that the discrepancies between the various versions can only result from oral transmission, minimising the part played by literary redactors.

We cannot be certain about the proto-Digeneid, although
there must have been someone who thought of the basic framework of the Digenis story, linking father and son, just as
there was probably someone who thought of the framework of
the *Odyssey*, linking son and father. Nor can we be certain
how far the Grottaferrata version resembles this putative
poem; the wide divergences between the various versions suggests a wide difference between these versions and any original. Oral transmission may have produced the confusion in
the Escorial version, but the other versions have few traces
of oral composition apart from a certain amount of muddle,
and some of the errors may be due to slovenly copying of a
literary text. It might seem that though *Digenis* does not
have many formulae or repeated lines it looks as if it might
have had them once. Thus when Digenis is fighting Kinnamos
we are told three times that he does not hit a fallen foe,
and each time a different phrase is used.[12] This sounds like
a deliberate avoidance of repetition, alteration for the
sake of alteration, a literary device very easy with a fluid
metre and the language in a fluid state; the ease with which
one version can slightly alter the sounds of another without
altering the sense makes the same point. Because the poem is
short and the metre easy to adapt there is not much need for
formulae in *Digenis* which cannot really be compared to Homer
with its difficult metre or to the South Slav epics where
the language is more rigid. The shorter *Chanson de Roland*
provides a better comparison, and here there are less
formulae. Thus the lack of formulae does not rule out oral
transmission, but there is a lot to be said for the idea of
several literary redactors ironing out the formulae, and
incidentally ironing out a good deal of sense from an originally orally composed Digeneid. The existence of akritic
songs, the reference in Arethas of Caesarea to cursed Paph-
logonians who now make up songs about the adventures of
famous men, the reference in Book V to Digenis telling his
adventures to a Cappodocian who appears in the poem rather
like Homer's ἀοιδός, and the muddle and confusion of the
poem suggest oral composition at an early stage, and the
absence of formulae suggests literary redactions.[13]

There is a danger that *Digenis* falls between two stools.
As an oral poem it obviously falls short of the splendid
simplicity and dignity of the Serbian poems, or even of Beowulf. As a written epic it clearly cannot compare with

Milton or Virgil. Provided we make due allowances for its
peculiar mixed status we are more likely to be charitable to
Digenis. The problem of whether we should regard *Digenis* as
an oral or literary epic crops up again when we look at a
third area into which a great deal of research has been done.
On the one hand we have the quotations and imitations from
the *Iliad*, Heliodorus and Achilles Tatius which look like
the work of the writer of literary epic; just as Virgil
quotes from Homer, and Dante from Virgil, so the author of
Digenis is keen to show his familiarity with other epics and
to place his work in the epic tradition.[14] On the other hand
we have the vaguer but more exciting similarities with other
epic and quasi-epic poems from East and West; the similarities are thematic rather than verbal, and seem to conjure up
a picture of Asia Minor, halfway between East and West acting as a kind of melting pot for ballad literature. The possible parallels are impressive; the Persian epic of *Firdausi*,
progenitor of Matthew Arnold's *Sohrab and Rustum*, the
Turkish epic of *Sidi Battal*, the *Arabian Nights*, the Serbian
and Bulgarian lays of Marko Kraljevic, and even the tenth
century Latin poem, written in Germany, entitled *Waltharius*
have all been cited.[15] The wide travels of *Digenis* need not
surprise us. A poem which began its life in Asia Minor as
The Bridge of Adana, travelled all over the Balkans in about
ten different languages, entitled *The Bridge of Area*, and
has been heard sung by gypsies in Morocco.[16] The poem telling of a river which could only be bridged when the wife of
the builder immured herself in the masonry, has the same
attitudes and same origins as *Digenis*.

Some of the parallels cited between *Digenis* and other
epics may seem a little far fetched; that with *Waltharius*
appears to rest on the common episode of the hero resting
his head in a maiden's lap, not, one would have thought, all
that an uncommon incident. On the other hand this kind of
parallel resulting from oral transmission would seem more
interesting than the literary parallels, especially as it is
disappointing that the parallels with Homer are few and far
between, the romances of Achilles Tatius and Heliodorus
being preferred. The Trebizond and Andros versions are the
only manuscripts actually to quote Homer, and they contain a
line where some monk has copied down the name Penelope as
Olope. The Grottaferrata version gets the name Penelope
right, but in general has not a great deal of time for Homer.
But Homeric scholars can certainly learn from *Digenis* by
looking into parallels with other epics; the Epic of Gilgamesh is an obvious case.[17] Some may be surprised that the
gap of a thousand years between Gilgamesh and Homer can be
bridged, although Gilgamesh was still being improved upon

two thousand years after its original composition. In this
connexion the hopes of Greeks in the 1920s that Digenis
would help them, and the fact that *Digenis* has as one of its
main characters a man called Philopappos who ruled Asia
Minor just before the Roman conquest of that province appear
comparatively small beer.

After all this scholarship there seems grave doubt among
those who should know about the poem's status and reputation.
Mavrogordato calls *Digenis* an epic throughout his introduc-
tions, but concludes by saying that the poem is in fact a
romance. On the whole he is on the side of the epic as
opposed to the ballads, since he says that a fourth-rate
ballad is superficially more attractive than a second-rate
epic.[18] Not so Trypanis who calls *Digenis* first a verse
romance, then a strange epic written by a feeble Byzantine
poet, far inferior to the ballads in which the real epic
spirit lies.[19] Politis says that the poem is neither a
romance nor a court epic, but a heroic epic, although he
admits that some of the heroic quality has been lost in the
literary redactions.[20] Entwistle[21] is very rude about
Digenis which he calls an epos, saying that the poet continues to outline dramatic situations which he continues to
foozle through sheer lack of a gift for narrative.

An epic should instruct, a romance should entertain; an
epic deals with the real, a romance with the ideal. The
Odyssey is more entertaining, more unrealistic and more of a
romance than the *Iliad*; how many wives preserve in real life
both their beauty and virtue for twenty years? Less easy to
define is the division between epic poems and heroic lays,
sagas, chansons de geste, narodne pesme, tragoudia or any of
the rich and varied terms which nations have used to describe
their local oral poetry. We look to an epic for some kind of
completeness, some kind of answer to the problems of destiny,
whereas a heroic lay provides at best a fragmentary insight
into the world around us. On both counts *Digenis* qualifies
as an epic, being instructive and real on the one hand, and
aiming at a full vision and complete answer on the other.
The trouble is that partly as a result of its small compass
the vision, the instruction and the answer provided by
Digenis are a little limited.

Some of the criticisms levelled against *Digenis* can be
easily rebutted. It is true that the story of the Emir is
worrying from the point of view of the narrative, but it is
also worrying for an escapist reader that the *Odyssey* spends
so much time on Telemachus before it gets on to Odysseus's
fairy tale adventures. The first person narrative of the
central books is seen by some as a mistake; it is argued
that we know that the events have happened, and therefore

there is no suspense, only a slight confusion about
Digenis's veracity as a narrator. These are trivial accusa-
tions, and it is odd that they do not seem to be levelled
against the *Aeneid* or the *Odyssey*, where the hero tells the
story of his greatest adventures.

A failure as a romance does not necessarily indicate
success as an epic, and here we have to turn to an examination of some of the positive features which qualify *Digenis*
for the title of an epic, albeit not a very good one, even
after making due allowance for the mangled state in which we
find the poem. But some of the claims for *Digenis*'s epic
status are misguided. *Digenis* is not an epic because it cele-
brates Greek national feeling. The idea that an epic is in
some sense an expression of national consciousness is a
relic of the struggle for national independence at the time
when new epics were being discovered at the end of the nineteenth century. Not many of the great epics are particularly
chauvinist; it is wrong for instance to dismiss Virgil as a
particularly patriotic writer, since he is obviously so much
more. In any case Digenis, the product of two races, fighting for his own sake, is hardly a model for narrow patriots.
As a reaction against this view we have the opinion that
what gives the poem unity and point is the idea that it is
celebrating peace and reconciliation, the goal to which the
multi-racial Byzantine empire was continually striving
during the time of the Macedonian dynasty and which it might
seem to have achieved at about the time *Digenis* was composed.
But Digenis seems an oddly warlike figure to be the hero of
a gospel of peace, and in spite of the odd pious insertion
he is not a very good spokesman for Christianity either.[22]

Unlike the *Chanson de Roland* and *Beowulf*, heroic lays,
which deal with one or two incidents, *Digenis* like the
Odyssey covers a full range of events and by means of the
introduction of the Emir widens his field by introducing
more than one central character. The Emir provides the easi-
est clue to the theme of *Digenis*. He is of mixed racial
stock, and this fact, together with his conversion to Christianity, has encouraged readers of the poem to think it is
concerned with the spreading of peaceful multi-racial Christianity. Neither Digenis, nor his father is a very satisfactory muscular Christian; those who praise the first section
of the epic as full of lively coherent narrative seem to
ignore the rather ghastly episode when the Emir for reasons
that are never satisfactorily explained tells his future
brothers-in-law that their sister is in a ditch with a lot
of lovely ladies chopped into little bits.[23] What Digenis
has in common with his father, and what shines through every
book of the epic is a burning love for his wife, a love that

enables him to conquer all adversaries, including his own mother, and to find a meaning for his own existence.

If love is the feature which gives meaning and purpose to the poem, it may look as if *Digenis* is a romance after all, since love is what gives point to most romances. But Digenis's love is a real one and owes nothing to romantic fantasy. It is a love which finds consummation in marriage, an unromantic notion, but not in children or in long old age, since God who can do all shows his compassion simply by allowing Digenis's wife to die before him. In this slightly naive attitude to God's power and in his praise of marriage Digenis seems to stand outside the Epic tradition, though well in the Byzantine tradition whose limitations I began by exploring. The major epics wrestle with the problems of God, free will and immortality; Digenis wrestles with bears, lions and Amazons, but is content to leave philosophical niceties to the theologians. In the major epics, apart from the *Odyssey* marriage does not seem very important to the heroes who have greater concerns. We do not hear much of Mrs Achilles, Aeneas's two wives are a pale shadow of his non-wife Dido, Dante's wife has to give way to Beatrice, and of the suggested heroes of *Paradise Lost* God, Christ and Satan are unmarried, while Adam and Milton are not very happily married. On the other hand Digenis's lonely struggle to preserve his married happiness does seem to achieve epic status.

NOTES

1. *Digenes Akritas*, edited with an introduction, translation and commentary by J. Mavrogordato (Oxford, 1956) and *The Two Blood Border Lord*, translated with an introduction and notes by D.B. Hull (Ohio, 1972). Mavrogordato gives a full if not recent bibliography.
2. Grottaferrata, 1.101.
3. Grottaferrata, 2.413.
4. Grottaferrata, 4.56 for Basil. Andros version, 1369 and Trebizond, 836 for Romanos. Andros, 4344 and Trebizond, 3107 for Nikephoros.
5. Mavrogordato, pp.xxxi, lxxi.
6. *The Ballads of Marko Kraljevic*, translated with an introduction by D.M. Low (Cambridge, 1922).
7. *Serbo-Croatian Heroic Songs*, collected by Milman Parry and edited by A.B. Lord, vol.1 (Harvard and Belgrade, 1954) p.110.
8. For a useful comparison between Roland and Digenis see H. Gregoire, *Autour de l'Epopee Byzantine* (London, 1975).

9. Well shown by J. Hagin, *The Epic Hero and the Decline of Epic Poetry*, (Bern, 1964).
10. Compare Grottaferrata, 4.27 'Παύσασθε γράφειν 'Όμηρον καὶ μύθους 'Αχιλλέως / ὡσαύτως καὶ τοῦ 'Έκτορος, ἄπερ εἰσὶ ψευδέα with *Paradise Lost*, 9. 13-47.
11. G. Morgan, 'Digenis in Crete', in Κρήτικα Χρόνικα 14 (1960) pp.44-68.
12. Grottaferrata, 6.264-9.
13. Mavrogordato, pp.xxvi-xxix.
14. Mavrogrodato, pp.lxxx and 265-6.
15. Mavrogordato, pp.lxxii-v, largely derived from Gregoire.
16. W. Entwistle, *European Balladry* (Oxford, 1934) p.315.
17. J. Griffin, *Homer on Life and Death* (Oxford, 1980) quotes some interesting parallels between Homer and Near Eastern myths.
18. Mavrogordato, p.xxviii.
19. C. Trypanis, *Medieval and Modern Greek Poetry* (Oxford, 1951) pp.xxv-xxviii.
20. L. Politis, *A History of Modern Greek Literature* (Oxford, 1973) pp.23-5.
21. Entwistle, p.304.
22. N.G. Polites, Περὶ τοῦ 'Έπους τῶν Νεωτέρων 'Ελλήνων (Athens, 1906) distorts Digenis into both a Christian and a national hero.
23. Grottaferrata, 1.224.

7 Children of Homer: the Epic Strain in Modern Greek Literature

PAUL MERCHANT

European writers of this century have not generally responded to their times through the medium of epic, and where
they have done so, they have been most successful in epic
theatre and novel. The confusion and despair expressed by
Eliot in *The Waste Land* has encouraged, as William Carlos
Williams had feared,[1] the development of the tentative and
the introspective as the characteristic voice of modern European poetry. Taking his hint from Whitman, Pound invented an
epic form which allowed for leaps and ellipses of subject-
matter and style, a form which answered to the increasing
complexity of his world; and Williams and Olson have continued that process. In their hands the long poem is an attempt
to respond to the full range of life's impact, a synthesis
of the influences of locality, tradition, culture, politics,
art.[2] In Europe, however, the strength of the lyric tradition had combined with our moral and ideological uncertain-
ties to produce the characteristic short personal poem,
limited to the description of the emotions attached to a
single event. There have, of course, been European poets of
larger scope; in Britain there were MacDiarmid, Bunting,
David Jones; and recently two shorthand versions of epics,
Geoffrey Hill's *Mercian Hymns* and Ted Hughes's *Crow*. A representative Eastern European example might be the Hungarian
Ferenc Juhasz, whose extended folk lament *The Boy Changed
into a Stag Clamours at the Gate of Secrets* begins with an
intense personal dialogue but expands into an inclusive
account of a lost world.[3] Yet these tend to be the excep-
tions in current writing. MacDiarmid gives the clearest description of the new role of epic, and at the same time an
explanation of its occasional inaccessibility, in his statement that 'the lyric, by its very nature, cannot reflect the
complexities of modern life. But apart from that, it necessarily ignores something even more important, and that is

the enormous new perspective of the sciences. That can't be encapsulated in a short lyric. It's because of that enormous variety (which ought to be the pre-occupation of poetry and so seldom is) that most modern poetry is trivial and worthless. . . . The epic is the only form which can discharge the duties of the poet in the modern world'.[4]

In Greece, however, with its almost unbroken tradition of the long poem, contemporary writers have frequently responded to the complexity of their times with epic, and most often with poetic epic, to produce a body of work expressive of the national, as well as personal, turmoils of this century. In some important respects the literature of Greece may be said to stand in as crucial a strategic position, in relation to continental writing, as the country has always been placed in politics by its geography. The Eastern Mediterranean has in the past been important as a crucible of ideas, and Greece continues to respond fully in its literature to the vagaries of its history.

This response is not necessarily innovative in its themes. Two of the most powerful voices in modern Greece, Kazantzakis and Seferis, have gone directly to the classical tradition for key motifs; for each of them the *Odyssey* has been a vital myth for their times. The 'centrifugal and experimental' hero of Kazantzakis[5] answers both to the versatility described in Homer's opening lines and also to the intellectual and cultural challenges of an expanded, multinational world. Kazantzakis wrote: 'so far as I am concerned, there has been no age more epical than ours. It is in such ages which come between two cultures - when one Myth dissolves and another struggles to be born - that epic poems are created'.[6] The man poised between the past and future, an energetically creative hero (who in the poem three times exposes the futility of decaying civilisations, those of Ithaka, Crete and Egypt, and attempts to reform each of them) is also a man between two cultures, East and West. In the words of Kazantzakis, 'Crete, for me (and not, naturally, for all Cretans) is the synthesis which I always pursue, the synthesis of Greece and the Orient. I neither feel Europe in me nor a clear and distilled classical Greece; nor do I at all feel the anarchic chaos and will-less perseverance of the Orient. I feel something else, a synthesis, a being that not only gazes on the abyss without disintegrating, but which, on the contrary, is filled with coherence, pride and manliness by such a vision.'[7] This Odysseus is a revolutionary, possessed by his ambition for a remade world, though his one successful creation, a new city, is destroyed by an earthquake during its inauguration. And paradoxically also the optimistic Marxism of the hero's purposes is expressed through a personality owing far more to the author's early influences, Nietzsche and Bergson; the replacement of a dying order is in the hands of a hero who finally faces death on an Antarctic iceberg. Yet these paradoxes are the essence of the poem; if this final episode on the iceberg is reminiscent of the isolated monster in Frankenstein, we are reminded also of the aspiration that led to the making of that monster. The interest of Kazantzakis's hero is that his isolation, so far from leaving us with a sense of impotence, rather makes this Odysseus a representative, just as the characters in the same author's novel *The Greek Passion* (*Christ Recrucified*), as villagers acting out a Passion Play, enter the roles that they are playing. At the climax of the novel Manolis, by now the suffering servant of the village, calls out before his death: 'If bolshevik means what I have in my spirit, yes, I am a bolshevik, Father; Christ and I are bolsheviks.'[8] This willingness to raise the individual to representative status takes many forms in the examples that follow.

In Seferis, altogether a more spare and restrained stylist, the ancient myths of Elpenor, Helen, the Argonauts, are frozen in a timeless present set in the landscape of modern Greece. Events from the distant past enter our world and hover in front of us, just as the female statue drawn out of the earth in Engomi floats in the air:

And the shepherd stayed with his crook uplifted in the air.
And I looked again at that ascending body;
Multitudes had assembled together, a swarm of ants,
And were striking her with spears and not hurting her.[9]

At such moments, when Seferis allows time to stand still, history seems to accuse us. This sense of stasis, of the failure of the modern world to do more than confront its heroic past, is common in the poetry of Seferis, and leaves an effect of disillusion and irony antithetical to the constant renewal in Kazantzakis. Yet the longing for a future to continue the work of the past is similar in both writers, and there is a strong feeling of exhaustion also in both, a sense of an intolerably heavy burden carried for too long. The poised moments in Seferis again make archetypes of ordinary people (as in the passage from 'Engomi', where the bystanders gather associations even of Christian iconography) but with less purpose than the allegorical types in Kazantzakis, who are the agents in a programme of action. In Seferis it is most often the world of the poem that is the most urgent focus of creation, rather than the world of life.

Yet this very activity, where an essentially lyric poet

chooses to set his moments of inspiration in the larger time-
frame of history, is itself an allegory, a statement that
individual perceptions are raised above the mundane by the
claim of a larger context, their place in a long-lived and
still developing culture. To that extent the work of Seferis
offers an optimistic position, even where it exposes the
failure of the present. At its most powerful, however, Epic
can be more than this. It is almost always the mode used by
a culture when it speaks authoritatively about its condition.
It is characteristically called up by moments of great crisis, where a culture defines itself or reaches one of the
geological faults of its history. In literary terms this may
be expressed in a heroic epic of combat, as the *Iliad* acts
as the literary expression of a wide scatter of cultural
relationships, between Greece as she was barely beginning to
define her national identity, and the civilisations on her
Eastern boundaries. At a later stage in Greek literature the
same characteristic mixture of curiosity about, and justifi-
able apprehension of, their near-Eastern neighbours were
expressed by Herodotus in a pioneering work of historical
investigation and by Aeschylus in a masterpiece of epic
theatre, but for the oral culture at the first moment of
impact, heroic epic was the means immediately to hand, and
the terms (and even some of the formal elements) of the
Iliad have tended to govern later Greek treatments of similar cultural issues, right up to the present, an influence
that is more than mere literary piety.

The other great theme, that of wandering and return, found
in the *Odyssey* in its purest form, may be seen also as the
germ of the Hellenistic Romances, with their enforced separ-
ations and reunions, and also of the great Quest narratives
and even of later picaresque novels; but more recently Greek
writers have seen in this myth an ideal expression of the
experience of exile, of the homeland viewed from a distance.
In the hands of Kazantzakis and Seferis this theme has already shown its versatility, allowing the former the widest
possible sweep of his net, and the latter the scrupulous objectivity of the self-exile. Both of these writers spent
many years outside Greece. Curiously, the themes of combat
and exile are both important in each of the Homeric epics,
with the *Iliad* describing a war fought at a distance (its
nostalgia emphasised by the 'Greek' feel of the similes) and
the *Odyssey* journey culminating in a trial of strength. It
is notable in this context that the great medieval epic hero,
Digenis Akrites, combines in his very title of Akrites the
two great themes, as a warrior who is also a border fighter;
his name Digenis, a reminder of his dual Saracen and Greek
parentage, reinforces this image. It may not, then, be

inappropriate to note that all the great writers of contemporary Greece have come from the borders of the Hellenic
world, and not, as one would expect, from the capital. Just
as the creation of the Homeric poems (as opposed to their
recension) has been located in the islands of Asia Minor or
in Sicily, but never in Athens, so Seferis, Elytis and
Vakalo are from Asia Minor, Palamas, Ritsos and Sinopoulos
are Peloponnesians, Kazantzakis a Cretan and Cavafy a Con-
stantinopolitan living in Alexandria. The vision of all
these writers was undoubtedly sharpened by the experiences
of border conflict, and by two traumatic events in particular, the defeat of the Greek army by the Turks in 1897 and
the later defeat of 1922, leading to the loss of Asia Minor
that sent one and a half million Greeks to the mainland as
refugees. Seferis has published a prose account of his
return visit to that lost world, a fierce anger burning
behind the elegant cadences: 'Nowadays it is a commonplace
to speak of the disasters of war. But it is even more painful to feel in your vitals the sudden disappearance of a
complete and living world, with its moments of light and of
shadow, its rituals of joy and sorrow, the closely woven
fabric of its whole existence: to hear in your ears the
cracking of its joints at the moment of its extinction. And
the shameful actions of that time.'10

The two great generations of modern Greek writers, the
'Generation of 1880' and the 'Turning Point' group of the
1930's, which took its name from the first volume of Seferis,
Strophe, published in 1931, have the disasters, of 1897 and
1922 respectively, at their shoulders. The great achievement
of the first generation, notably that of Costis Palamas and
Constantine Cavafy, was the creation not only of a literary
language but also of a sense of Hellenism. The 'language
question', the relentless debate between the invented purist
Katharevousa and the naturally evolved Demotic, still haunts
modern Greek letters. But the publication of The Twelve Lays
of the Gipsy by Palamas in 1907 established Demotic as the
authentic poetic language, if for no other reason than for
the range of its vocabulary and idiom. Set in Constantinople
at the great gathering of Gipsies for their May Day celebra-
tion, written from the view-point of the oppressed wanderers
and placed in time shortly before the Fall of Constantinople,
it is a semi-programmatic account of the renewable elements
in Greek culture. Palamas finds strength in the virtuosity
and adaptability of the Gipsies; he allows the Akrites in
Canto 8 to prophesy the decline of the city and of heroic
Hellenism:

The soul of Romiosini, Digenis, is gone for ever,
    swallowed up in the shadows of the earth without a
    shroud.
Gone, O Romiosini, is the hero whom you exalted above
    thrones and palaces, your king of kings.
Gone is his watch-tower, too, your crowning glory and
    protection,
That square-based octagon, which, through its embrasures
    manned by fighting-men,
Commanded all the plains, like a peak perennially snow-
    covered,
From Babylon to Syria, from Taurus and Antitaurus as far
    as Lebanon,
From the citadels of Tarsus to the caliphates of Baghdad.[11]

Yet the Gipsy folk-tale of Sir Tearless and Lady Laughter-
less in Canto 11 is presented as an image of the new driving
force that will replace the decadent civilisation, in a disturbing marriage of power and wisdom, identified by George
Thomson as 'that combination of private enterprise and scientific knowledge which is the driving force of capitalist
society. . . . The union of art and magic was necessarily
unproductive. Only modern industry can create the material
conditions for the emancipation of mankind'.[12] Canto 11
closes with the poem's clearest optimistic statement, in
imagery as reminiscent of Penelope as of Odysseus:

I am forerunner of the people which comes, goes, and never
    rests,
Untouched, unattached, undismayed,
Which, though it never seems to change, is weaving slowly
    in the night-time
Changes that shall transform the world.[13]

The poem's two-canto coda confirms this optimism in a message to the poet delivered in solitude by Nature, and in a
personal dedication 'To a Woman'. The work ends quietly, but
its effect is ambitious, and convincing, an image of inclu-
siveness, justified in its confidence that poetry can be a
medium of progressive change. Though it has few features in
common with Virgil's epic, it could be said to perform the
same function of giving a voice to national aspiration - in
this case literally, as well as figuratively.
    Another provincial view of Hellenism, again with the
objectivity of the outsider, came from Cavafy. In 'Philhellene', written in 1906, an Eastern king is giving
instructions for the design of a new coin. The poem ends:

Above all I beg you, take care
(as you fear God, Sithaspis, keep this in mind)
that after King and Preserver
is carved in neat characters Philhellene.
Now don't start your litany
of "Greeks? Where?" or "What is there Greek
Here beyond the Zagros, over the Euphrates?"
So many more barbarous than ourselves
have dared write this, that we shall do no less.
Lastly, remember that at times
sophists have come here from Syria,
poetasters, and other pedants.
So we are not unhellenized, I trust.[14]

The finely judged irony here qualifies, but does not make
absurd, such pride and aspiration at the borders of the
Hellenic world. History for Cavafy is a teacher, and inspiration, more than a burden; there is a melancholy present,
but in his choice of multiple personae from the past (even
if most commonly from the Hellenistic or Greco-Roman past)
the poet takes on a large role, one verging on the heroic.
The title 'Philhellene' confers responsibilities. We shall
see a similar shouldering of responsibility in Ritsos's use
of history.

The generation of the 1930s, many of whom are still writing, have experienced times of considerable stress. The
literary life of Greece was much changed by the Albanian
campaign, the German war-time Occupation and the post-war
Civil Wars. Three poets, Odysseus Elytis, Takis Sinopoulos
and Yannis Ritsos, have produced a genuinely heroic poetry
of Resistance. The *Heroic and Elegiac Song for the Dead
Second Lieutenant of Albania* (1945) and parts of *Worthy it
Is* (1959), both by Elytis, confront the agonies of the
decade of war, and set alongside them the realisation of a
common purpose.[15] That this unity of spirit was not easily
translated into political terms is shown by the instability
of successive governments from Metaxas to the Colonels, and
the uneasy truce that has followed, but the conviction and
inspiration of *Heroic and Elegiac Song* is authentic enough:

The trees are of coal which the night cannot kindle.
The wind runs wild beating its breast, the wind still
      beating its breast
nothing happens. Forced to their knees the mountains roost
under the frost. And roaring out of the ravines,
out of the heads of the dead rises the abyss . . .
Not even Sorrow weeps any longer. Like the mad orphan girl

she roams about, wearing on her breast a small cross of
     twigs
but does not weep. Surrounded only by pitch-black
     Acroceraunia
she climbs to the summit and sets the moon's disk there -
perhaps the planets will turn and see their shadows
and hide their rays
and stand poised
breathless with amazement at chaos . . .

The wind runs wild beating its breast, the wind still
     beating its breast
the wilderness is muffled in its black shawl
crouching behind months of cloud it listens
what is there to listen for, so many cloud-months away?
With a tangle of hair on her shoulders - ah, leave her
     alone -
half a candle half a flame a mother weeps - leave her
     alone -
in the chill empty rooms where she roams leave her alone!
For fate is never a widow
and mothers are here to weep, husbands to fight
orchards for the breasts of girls to blossom
blood to be spent, waves to break into foam
and freedom to be born always in the lightning flash![16]

There is a powerful, and I think realistic, mixture here of
fatalism and idealism, carried on an unusual degree of
rhetoric. The symbolist/surrealist manner no doubt owes as
much to the French tradition as to any, but there are demotic
Greek folk motifs here also, and there is nothing absurd in
this raising of the unnamed officer's death to the status of
myth. As in Seferis, time has stopped, and Nature turns to
watch the event, but the effect here is to enlarge, not
diminish, the present, to create a more than mundane figure
about whom Creation, for this important instant, revolves.
     Takis Sinopoulos has also read widely in French Symbolist
writing, and has translated contemporary French poets. His
Deathfeast (1968), a compressed, incantatory lament for the
dead of the Civil Wars, originated in a shorter poem, *Deathfeast for Elpenor* (1946) directly influenced by the calling
of the souls in *Odyssey* 11. This part of the *Odyssey*, where
some of the dead heroes of the *Iliad* return in a new context,
has been a powerful image, for Seferis as well as Sinopoulos,
of a moment where heroic ideals are evaluated in a domestic
context. In this version the roll-call of dead names calls
up both horrific memories and glimpses of happiness from the
same years. The poem begins calmly, in resignation:

A wave of tears scorched me. What was I, years speaking
     with,
years alone reviving lost faces and through the window
     came
glory shaded gold light, all around benches and tables and
mirrors, windows to the underworld. And they came
dismounting one after the other
Porporas, Kontaxis, Markos, Gerasimos
thick hoar-frost the horses and the day swerving
through the numb air. Bilias came, and Gournas,
gipsies outlined on the dusk, and Phakalos,
carrying mandoline, guitar, flute -
the sound easing the spirit, the house indoors fragrant
for months with rain and wood. And they lit
only when they lit the fire hot to get warm
I called out to them cheerfully.

As the memories crowd in, so the conscience bites; but the
poet scrupulously records the facts:

Old men came and children.
In their thin clothes how could they stand firm
how could children grow in such horror -
the old men creaking, too tall for their bodies,
and the children
carrying axe, knife, hatchet
in their eyes contempt and menace now, and they said
     nothing.

Trenches, refuse-dumps, mothers howling, terrible and
     black, whom did
you kill, they asked again and again, and you, whom did
     you kill, how
many did we kill?

But at the close of the poem a kind of absolution has been
won, and the emotion is channelled into images of renewal:

Then came the days of forty four
and the days of forty eight.
And from the Peloponnese to Larissa,
to the depths of Kastoria,
on the map a black infection,
Greece constricted, panting -
at Easter we counted in deserted Kozani
how many were left above, how many had gone down
the dark river.

Prosoras came, holding his broken rifle,
Bakrisioris, Alafouzos, Zervos
joined the gathering. Look, I shouted, we looked,
the light flooding, the fruitful sun.
Years have passed, we have gone grey, I told them
Tsepetis came, Zafoglou, Markoutsas
settled down on the bench and
at the end Konstantinos nursing his foot.

One by one the voices grew quiet
one by one as they had come they left.
They walked down the valley, breaths of air, they left.
For the last time I watched them, called out to them.
The fire sank to the ground and through the window came

How a single star makes the night sky navigable

As an unknown soldier lies in an empty church
anointed among the flowers.[17]

The poem stands with *Romiosini* of Yannis Ritsos; these are
the definitive modern statements of the survival of human
values in times of war. *Romiosini* (*Greekness*) is the outstanding demotic poem, an outpouring of popular energy:

These trees are out of place under a smaller sky
these stones are out of place under a stranger's tread
these faces are out of place except under the sun
these hearts are out of place except under justice.

This land is as severe as silence
hugging its charred stones to its body
hugging its orphaned olives and vines in the light
clenching its teeth. There is no water. Only light.
The road is lost in the light and the sheepfold's shadow
    is iron.

Trees, rivers and voices turn to marble in the sun's glare.
The root stumbles on the marble. The gum trees are dusty.
Mule and rock. Parched. Since time began. They all chew
    mouthfuls of sky to stifle their bitterness.

Their eyes are red with sleeplessness
a deep furrow driven between their eyebrows
like a cypress between two mountains at sunset.

Their hands are welded to the rifle
the rifle a continuation of their hands

their hands a continuation of their souls -
they hold their anger at their lips
they hold their pain deep, deep in their eyes
like a star in a brine-pit.

When they clasp hands the sun shines square on the world
when they smile a tiny swallow flies out of their savage
    beards
when they sleep twelve stars fall from their empty pockets
when they are killed life sweeps uphill with banners and
    drums.

These opening lines are perhaps the best known in modern
Greek; the fourth line appeared as a caption to a front-page
photograph of striking building workers in an Athens news-
paper eight days before the Colonels' coup, in which Ritsos
was arrested, not for the first time. The terms here are
taken from landscape and the human figure (trees, stones,
faces, hearts); the questions are moral and political. The
poem is built from images that might as easily refer to
Missolonghi in 1821, or to Digenis, as to soldiers of the
Second World War or First Civil War, but the poet is careful
to leave the tense of every verb in the present, and most of
the poem's concerns are timeless. Ritsos uses the heroic and
the legendary alongside the contemporary and the particular,
since for him heroism is not only possible, but expected, in
the modern world. To inherit tradition, he suggests, is to
take responsibility for continuing it:

The hour swells to a summer Saturday night in the sailors'
    bar
night swells to a baking dish on the tinker's wall
the song swells like a loaf for a sponge-diver's supper
and there the Cretan moon trundles its great wheel.
Clack! Clack! Twenty rows of hobnails in their high
    leather boots
there they go climbing the stone staircase of Nafplion
filling their pipes with thick-cut leaves of darkness
their moustaches the star-spattered thyme of Roumeli
their teeth a pine root deep in the Aegean's crags and
    salt.

They have passed through iron and fire, spoken with rocks
served Death with wine from their grandfathers' skulls
they have met with Digenis on the same threshing-floor
and sat down to eat
breaking their pain like barley loaves across their
    knees.[18]

There could be no clearer statement of the continuity of the heroic tradition.

Yet the epic in contemporary Greece has not been confined to heroic subject-matter. Between the dictatorships of Metaxas and the Colonels more domestic concerns predominated, in some respects a greater challenge for the writer, just as comedy is harder to write than tragedy. The poet's task, even the epic poet's, is to raise the ordinary in everyday life to significance, in peace as much as in war. Homer's descriptions of domestic life in Ithaca, Sparta and Phaeacia (and for that matter, Troy) are among his most characteristic work, the most direct test of his intentions as a poet. The accurate portrayal of the norm in a society is very hard to achieve, and asks for both wide understanding and directness and simplicity of expression. These are not always found together, and 'primitive' artists often succeed where the more cultured have failed. Speaking of Makriyannis, the uneducated general who directed the War of Independence, Seferis comments: 'I was saying that Makriyannis is one of the most cultivated souls of the Greek world, and I should say the same thing of Theophilos [a 'primitive' painter], if the word 'culture' carries the meaning of spiritual form . . . for a training in life one can learn much from people like Theophilos who have worked in the dark but found their way searching along the dark passage of what is, I believe, a very cultivated collective soul - the soul of our people.'[19] It is in this sense that an oral epic culture can still be seen to exist. In Britain the most lively remaining oral tradition is in the theatre. Speaking in defence of the presentation of Howard Brenton's *The Romans in Britain*, Edward Bond argued: 'Each epoch creates its own humanity by asking the old question "What is Man?" and developing the rational and moral disciplines to answer it. Scientists and philosophers do this - and so do we all whenever we ask what we are doing with our lives. It is precisely because of this that drama is important. It examines the question as it is posed to ordinary people. That is why the freedom of the theatre is so vital.'[20] This free expression of the genuine in our culture, which Bond finds in the theatre, appears in Greece most naturally in the poets. Markos Avgheris, writing in 1945, called for a poetry of resistance in these terms: 'The mission of art is to include within a larger synthesis the feelings and desires of the people, to become the epic poem of its struggle.'[21] In recent years Ritsos has increasingly moved away from the public personae of large-scale poems like *Romiosini* towards a briefer, more compressed medium suitable to a time of comparative peace. Two sequences

of short poems, significantly entitled *Testimonies*, appeared
in 1963 and 1966, whose qualities the poet summarised as a
'silent gratitude towards human life, thought and art, before all trials and death - perhaps even in spite of them.'[22]
He gives himself a large canvas, with nothing excluded.
Perhaps we should see this as his Ithaca. I have taken an
example from each collection. The first presents the poet as
messenger to an uncomprehending and unappreciative world:

Alone with his work

All night he galloped alone, in wild excitement,
    pitilessly spurring
his horse's flanks. They were waiting for him, he said,
    undoubtedly,
there was great urgency. When he arrived at dawn
no-one was waiting, there was no-one. He looked all around.
Desolated houses, bolted. They were asleep.
He heard beside him his horse panting -
foam on his mouth, sores on his ribs, his back flayed.
He hugged his horse's neck and began to weep.
The horse's eyes, large, dark, near to death,
were two towers standing alone, far away, in a land where
    it was raining.

The poet speaks not as an individual but as a representative;
and after finishing his task, in circumstances much like
failure, the rider-poet hugs his horse-poem as between them
they confront the two conditions that have almost destroyed
them both: the difficulty of the work and the indifference
of the audience. In the second example, from the 1966 volume,
Ritsos returns to the *Odyssey* for the most basic images of
existence:

Insignificant details

When Eumaeus, the swineherd, stood up to receive
the stranger that the sheepdogs had announced,
there fell from his knees the beautiful, finely-worked
    oxhide
that he was preparing for his sandals. Later,
as they went to slaughter the two pigs
for the old man's dinner of welcome, he tightened his belt.
These - the hide, his sandals, the tightening of the belt -
their secret meaning (beyond gods and myths,
beyond symbols and concepts) only poets understand.[23]

In both these short poems there is a movement from the

particular to the general, the discovery of a permanent
truth in the small-scale and the temporary. The restraint
and self-discipline shown here are not evidence of a diminu-
tion of power; on the contrary, they are an attempt to provide the irreduceable elements of a general truth - accuracy
taking the place of amplitude. It is here, at least as much
as in his longer poems, that Ritsos makes an epic claim, for
the long-term and large-scale importance of individual
details in a representative life, whether that of Eumaeus or
of a contemporary Greek. It is as if in these short poems
Ritsos is offering the similes taken from a larger, unspoken
epic, that of the whole history of Greece.

My final example, Eleni Vakalo, whose early work was surrealist, has recently written two extended sequences in the
folk tradition of her birthplace - the islands of the Eastern Aegean. The first, *Genealogy* (1971), is a collection of
reminiscences of her family, from ancestors to her own
generation, of her friends and neighbours, interwoven with
folk tales and snatches of song. Apparently artless, the
poem has the natural harmony of a peasant quilt, and the
final effect is far from naive. Its very simplicity is a
statement of homage, to those values that can be lost and
are worth preserving. 'But the poem is not a retrospective
act of memory', the poet records in her Introduction; 'it is
made up of features formed in our common roots, in our own
elementary behaviour. It is a conscious reworking of mythology'. *Genealogy* ended with the death of the poet's grand-
mother; the later poem, *About the World* (*Tou Kosmou*), published in 1978, carries the weight of further tragedy. The
brighter peasant colours have darkened; the concerns are
wider, more sombre and experienced, and at the same time
more inward-facing, returning again and again to the psychology of friendship and family ties, and to her own interior
landscape. The book is enigmatic, compressed and elliptical,
but even at its most difficult it speaks with a strange
lyrical music. It is clearly also epic in intention, not
only as a continuation of *Genealogy* but also in its particular objectives, to record the passage of substantial stret-
ches of time in her own life. One device for this is in the
reworking of poems from *The Forest*, published in 1954. The
earlier poems, printed in italic, are interlined with the
poet's later commentary from a distance of twenty years. One
of the poems treated in this way, 'My Father's Eye', had
been perhaps her best known; it is a surrealist joke, a fantasy. The accompanying commentary is starkly realist, steep-
ed in the experience of loss.[24] Yet its conclusion, in its
resignation and its insistence on perseverance, its long
perspective, is characteristic of the best in modern Greek

writing, clearly marking one of the paths along which the
epic should develop in our time:

Commentary

My Father's Eye, written exactly twenty years ago.

My father had a glass eye
My friend had only one breast

On Sundays spent at home he would take other eyes
from his pocket, polish them on the edge of his sleeve and
call to my mother to choose
My mother would laugh
My mother laughed quietly, I imagine now, after
twenty years, knowing the nostalgia of a child at my
nipple

Every morning my father was in good spirits
He would roll his eye in his palm before putting
it in, and would say what a good eye it was
My parents took up arms
In place of her breast my mother has, on the
bowstring side, an ugly scar

But I didn't want to believe him
What importance did I have in their life?

I would throw a dark shawl over my shoulders as if
I were cold so I could watch him secretly
The shadow that fell across our house from that
time on was myself

At last the day came when I saw him crying
There was no difference from a real eye
My mother - to tell the truth, I put my friend in
her place - has many other things to cry about

I spoke of growth; you must accept it

NOTES

1. *The Autobiography of William Carlos Williams* (New York, 1967) p.174.
2. Ezra Pound *The Cantos* (New York and London, 1930-70); William Carlos Williams, *Paterson* (New York and London, 1946-58); Charles Olson, *Maximus* (New York, 1953, 1960;

London, 1968).

3. Hugh MacDiarmid, *A Drunk Man Looks at the Thistle*
   (London, 1926); Basil Bunting, *The Spoils* (London, 1951),
   Briggflatts (London, 1965; David Jones, *Anathemata*
   (London, 1952); Geoffrey Hill, *Mercian Hymns* (London,
   1971); Ted Hughes, *Crow* (London, 1970); Ferenc Juhasz,
   *The Boy Changed into a Stag Clamours at the Gate of
   Secrets*, transl. David Wevill (Harmondsworth, 1970).

4. Hugh MacDiarmid, *Metaphysics and Poetry*, Lothlorian Pub-
   lications (Hamilton, 1975) pp.10-11.

5. W.B. Stanford, *The Ulysses Theme* (Oxford, 1963) p.223.

6. Nikos Kazantzakis, *The Odyssey* (Athens, 1938), transl.
   Kimon Friar (New York, 1959) p. xii.

7. Kimon Friar, Introd., Kazantzakis, *The Odyssey* (New York,
   1959) p.xix.

8. Nikos Kazantzakis, *Christ Recrucified*, transl. Jonathan
   Griffin (London, 1962) p.463.

9. George Seferis, *Poems*, transl. Rex Warner (London, 1960)
   p.121.

10. George Seferis, 'The Other World', transl. Ian Scott-
    Kilvert, *London Magazine*, VI, 5 (1966) 62.

11. Kostis Palamas, *The Twelve Lays of the Gipsy*, transl.
    George Thomson (London, 1969) p.107.

12. Palamas, *Twelve Lays*, p.22.

13. Palamas, *Twelve Lays*, p.131.

14. Constantine Cavafy, 'Philhellene', *Poems I* (Athens, 1963)
    p.37, transl. Paul Merchant.

15. Odysseus Elytis, *The Axion Esti*, transl. Edmund Keeley
    and George Savidis (London, 1980).

16. Odysseus Elytis, *Heroic and Elegiac Song 7*, transl. Paul
    Merchant, *Modern Poetry in Translation 4* (London, 1968);
    repr. Alan Bold (ed.), *Penguin Book of Socialist Verse*
    (Harmondsworth, 1970), pp.343-4.

17. Takis Sinopoulos, *Deathfeast*, transl. Paul Merchant,
    M.P.T.4 (London, 1968) from MS.; revised text (Athens,
    1972) transl. John Stathatos, Oasis Books (London, 1975).

18. Yannis Ritsos, *Romiosini*, (Athens, 1966), transl. Paul
    Merchant. The full poem, transl. Eleftherios Parianos,
    Penguin Book of Socialist Verse (Harmondsworth, 1970)
    pp.312-29.

19. George Seferis, *On the Greek Style*, transl. Rex Warner
    and Th. D. Frangopoulos (London, 1966) pp.37 and 7.

20. Edward Bond, '"The Romans" and the Establishment's Fig-
    leaf', *Guardian*, 4 November, 1980.

21. Kostas Myrsiades, 'Yannis Ritsos and Greek Resistance
    Poetry', *Journal of the Hellenic Diaspora* V, 3 (1978)
    47-56.

22. Myrsiades, 54.

23. Yannis Ritsos, 'Alone with his Work', 'Insignificant
    Details', *Testimonies 1 & 2* (Athens, 1963 and 1966),
    transl. Paul Merchant, *M.P.T.4* (London, 1968).
24. Eleni Vakalo, *Genealogy* (Athens and Exeter, 1971) transl.
    Paul Merchant (Interim Press, 1977); *About the World*
    (Athens, 1978) transl. Paul Merchant.

8 Postscript

TOM WINNIFRITH

Epic poems do not have postscripts. The *Iliad* ends with the
funeral of Hector, tamer of horses, and the *Aeneid* with the
pitiful death of Turnus; the *Odyssey* ends not with Odysseus's triumph, nor with the gibbering ghosts of the suitors,
but with Athena's intervention in the non-battle between the
suitors' relatives and the forces of Odysseus. *Paradise Lost*
concludes with Adam and Eve taking their solitary way
through Eden with wandering steps and slow. The epic note in
Tolstoy's *Anna Karenina* is admirably shown when the novel
does not cease on the high note of Anna's death, but with
the apparently mundane detail of Vronsky going off to fight
in Bulgaria, plagued by toothache. The epic's ability to
compass anything and everything is well illustrated by the
deliberately flat conclusions of the great epics.

This collection of essays does, however, need a postscript.
Epic features are found in Greek tragedy by Professor Gould,
in a variety of English authors by Professor Bayley, and in
modern Greek poetry by Mr. Merchant. Each makes an excellent
case, but those just beginning a study of the epic might
feel a little baffled by the meaning of the term epic. It is
in an attempt to help such students that this rather flat
postscript has been written.

The vast sea of literary criticism is littered with the
wrecks of literary terms that have once served some useful
purpose, but now stand as derelict hulks only serving to
trap the unwary traveller. Terms like classical, romantic
and lyrical once meant something, but now so many generations of critics have swept over their bows that almost
nothing of their former dignity or usefulness remains. The
good ship epic is in a slightly different category, perhaps
because of its vast size, perhaps because it has sailed in
such strange waters. Even if we know very little about literature we know that the *Iliad*, the *Odyssey*, the *Aeneid*, the

Divine Comedy and *Paradise Lost* are epic poems, and once
this is established we can make other definitions. *The Rape
of the Lock* is a mock epic poem, *War and Peace* and *Ulysses*
are novels with an epic quality, the *Book of Job* and *Gilgamesh* are near epics. It is fairly easy to reject other candidates as unworthy of being called epics; an epic is not
just a long poem dealing with a philosophical subject like
The Prelude, or a long poem dealing with adventure and chiv-
alry like *Idylls of the King*.

Virgil's *Aeneid* is consciously modelled on Homer's two
poems. There are in the *Aeneid* funeral games, single combats,
lists of combatants, conclaves of gods, tricks of style and
actual lines that are clearly borrowed from the *Iliad* or the
Odyssey. Dante takes Virgil as his guide through Inferno and
Purgatorio, and again, though the structure of the *Divine
Comedy* is different from that of Virgil and Homer's epics
with no battles or long similes and at times a deliberate
avoidance of the heroic, the whole idea of a descent into
the underworld is enlarged from the central book of the
Aeneid, itself an enlargement of and adaptation from an episode in the *Odyssey*. The theme of the quest is another
reminder of Homer. The Renaissance epics of Boiardo, Ariosto,
Camoes, Tasso and Spenser are recognisable descendants of
Homer and Virgil, and are also closely reminiscent of each
other. *Paradise Lost* is full of echoes of all previous epics,
though with its twelve books, long similes and ponderous
proper names it seems closest to Virgil and Homer.

It would seem then to be a feature of literary epics that
they are self-consciously imitative. We do not find other
poets copying their predecessors in the same way, or, if we
do, we do not think of them as great poets; Wordsworth and
T.S. Eliot are great because they break away from an established tradition, not because they follow one. And of course
great epic poets are original, very often overturning their
predecessors' values while apparently imitating them. Thus
Turnus and Satan, brave and brutal heroes in the Achilles
mould, turn out to be the villains of their particular
pieces, although such is the influence of Homer that we are
attracted to these villains, and feel that Virgil and Milton
were attracted too.

A lack of originality and too much conscious imitation
produces the sterile second rate epics of silver age Latin
and the eighteenth century in England. It is difficult to
know when epic poems become so bad that they cease to be
epics at all. Silius Italicus and Sir Richard Blackmore presumably count as writers of epic, though nobody reads them,
whereas the epic writers who so annoyed Juvenal in his first
satire sound so bad that we can hardly count them as poets.

The study of inferior epics does suggest that they failed
because lacking any original vision their authors fell back
on stock epic devices which were unsuited to their time or
theme. Conclaves of gods and single combats by heroes played
little part in the real Punic war or in seventeenth and
eighteenth century England. The steadiness and resilience of
the Roman legions allowed no time for individual heroics,
and the rumble and thunder of the blunderbuss made the clash
of shield against shield anachronistic: both Blackmore and
Silius Italicus waver uncertainly between anachronism and an
unwillingness to break out of the epic mould.[1]

Very different from these failed literary epics are the
near epic Serbian ballads. Dr Murray has said that the Yugoslavs have had their day, and modern students of Homer take
the line that we study the Serbian lays not to find out what
Homer is, but what he is not. This is a refreshing change
from the reverence resulting from the researches of Lord and
Parry which have tended to raise the status of such poems to
the dignity of a full blown epic. It is common to find
writers on Balkan poetry referring to quite short oral compositions as epics. Thus an excellent modern study of Yugoslav heroic poetry is entitled *The Making of the Epic*, even
though its Yugoslav author unlike most British students of
Yugoslav poetry is anxious to establish different levels of
quality in the heroic poems.[2] Songs, whether of the Kosovo
cycle, or those dealing with Marko Kraljevic, or later songs
about the wars of independence against the Turks, approach
epic quality if they are able to adapt the splendour of the
medieval bugaristice to their own subject and more humble
decasyllabic metre. They fail if they are unable to fuse the
natural with the supernatural, the medieval with the more
modern, the tragic with the comic, the historical with the
mythical.

Most students of Yugoslav oral poetry tend to give prece-
dence to the Kosovo cycle as being more noble and therefore
more epic than the lays about Marko Kraljevic or the wars
against the Turks. Equally the Serbian songs about Marko are
generally considered superior to their Bulgarian counter-
parts, not normally regarded as being epic at all. Without
disputing the validity of these judgements it is possible,
especially in the light of Professor Bayley's essay, to cast
doubt on the Arnoldian doctrine of high seriousness as a
criterion for the epic. The Kosovo cycle with its mournful
insistence on Prince Lazar's choice of a heavenly kingdom as
opposed to an earthly one is more high minded than the
accounts of Marko's drunken antics, but this does not make
the Kosovo songs more epic. There are moments of rude humour
in all the major epics, even in Virgil, whose funeral games

have a comic as well as a tragic side. The discomfiture of
Thersites, Hephaistus catching Aphrodite in bed with Ares,
Dante's devil making a bugle with his breech, and Milton's
crude jibes against Catholic friars are sufficient reminders
that the epic includes the low as well as the high, and that
it is the wholeness of the epic vision which the Kosovo
cycle lacks.

The feeling that the epic has a special nobility of
subject-matter and dignity of style is not confined to
Matthew Arnold or to admirers of the Kosovo lays. Horace
contrasts his humble satires written in prose that scans
with the full blown pride of epic poetry, although it may be
that he is mocking bad epic through the empty resonance of
the lines:

> neque enim quivis horrentia pilis
> agmina nec fracta pereuntis cuspide Gallos
> aut labentis equo describat vulnera Parthi.[3]

Pope in his preface to the *Iliad* is full of praise for
Homer's inventive fire, and dismisses the 'grosser represen-
tations of the Gods and imperfect manners of his heroes' as
more trivial faults. In his postscript to the *Odyssey* he con-
fesses to some difficulty in finding ways in which he can
'dignify and solemnise these plainer parts of his original',
and says he had imitated the style of Milton to cope with the
difficulty. Since he both imitates and cites Milton in the
Dunciad it may be that Pope is aware that the nobility of
the epic and the baseness of the anti-epic are not all that
easy to separate. Certainly there is an epic quality about
the *Dunciad*, just as there is an anti-epic note in *Paradise
Lost*.[4]

Arnold's other criteria for rescuing Homer from ignorant
translators like F.H. Newman are rapidity, directness and
simplicity. Unlike nobility these qualities clearly do not
apply to epic writers other than Homer. As Mr Gransden has
shown, Virgil operates indirectly by means of the parallels
with Homer, and the tortuous unwinding of his complex narrative with its carefully planned web of reverberating images
is an obvious contrast to Homer's direct approach, although
it may seem odd that Homer should be praised for simplicity
and rapidity. Professor Kirk's account of the *Diomedeia*
shows how far from simple Homer can be, and the first seven
books of the *Iliad*, if not the whole *Iliad*, can be seen not
as a rapid series of battles, but as cruel trickery on the
part of the gods whereby the inevitable fate that awaits
first the Greeks, then Hector, is cunningly delayed.

Writers of bad epics in the seventeenth century and bad

epic theorists in the nineteenth century liked to think that
an epic ought to celebrate a nation's glory. Thus to describe a poem as a national epic, involves not a paradox but
a tautology. Virgil's *Aeneid* is in some sense a national
epic, and some poems, notably Camoës's *Lusiads*, have succeeded in adapting Virgil's patriotic message to other
nations. Milton toyed with and Blackmore fell for a poem
celebrating Britain's mythical past. In the nineteenth century the rise of national consciousness led to an inflation
of certain poems to epic status because of their close connexion with a particular nation. Vuk Karadzic, the pioneer
recorder of many a Serbian lay, was a fervent Serbian nation-
alist who virtually created the Serbo-Croatian language as a
result of his literary researches.[5] In the Balkan wars Serbian soldiers kissed the soil of Kosovo, and in the First
World War they imagined that Marko Kraljevic fought on their
side. But these incidents, though moving, do not make Serbian
oral poetry into epics, any more than Finnish pride and the
ingenious work of Lönnrot in stitching the *Kallevala* together
makes this great collection of poems into a true epic.[6]

A study of true epics works against the theory that they
are confined to a narrow nationalistic view. Homer dominates
ancient Greek literature, and most Athenian waiters can
still recite the first line of the *Iliad* and the *Odyssey*,
but it is grossly unfair to Hector as well as to Homer to
say that the poet is on the side of the Greeks as opposed to
the side of humanity. Virgil was commissioned to write a
poem celebrating Augustus's triumphs and the Roman imperial
mission, and there are certain passages notably in Book 6
which do seem narrowly chauvinistic and which were popular
at times when imperial missions were in fashion. Today is
not such a time, and today we are able to see other aspects
of Virgil's many sided genius, most obviously in his sympathy for Dido and Turnus, obstacles in the way of Rome's or
Italy's progress. I have shown the absurdity of making
Digenis with his mixed racial and religious origins a cham-
pion of Greek orthodoxy. Dante is the poet of Italy almost
by accident, the accident being that the dialect of Florence
in which he wrote became standard Italian. His poem does
speak vaguely in favour of Italy for which Euryalus, Nisus
and Turnus and Camilla died, and against stepmotherly Florence,[7] and this early praise of a nation state as opposed
to a city state, analogous to Virgil and Augustus's propa-
ganda in favour of Italy as opposed to Rome, might seem to
lend some support to the idea of the *Divine Comedy* being a
national epic. But politics, though important for both
Virgil and Dante, is not all important, and Milton, Crom-
well's Latin secretary, had abandoned political ambitions by

the time he had abandoned the idea of a national epic.

Again in the post-Miltonic age epic theory and epic practice were dominated by the idea of the hero. An epic should
have a hero, and a hero should be perfect, it was thought;
hence Dryden's embarrassment with Aeneas's lapses from grace
in his translation of the *Aeneid*, rather less honest than
Pope's embarrassment with Achilles in his translation of the
Iliad. The failure of both Dryden and Pope to write epics of
their own is at least partly due to the failure of their age
to produce epic heroes. The amorous Stuarts and the fat Hano-
verians, prosperity at home and peace abroad, Capability
Brown and Inigo Jones are not the stuff of which heroes are
made. Gradually writers realised that a perfect hero could
not be found, and turned to the novel whose central characters like Moll Flanders and Tom Jones, attractive though
they were, are found in far from heroic postures.

The fact that traditionally heroes had found the chief
outlet for their heroism in battle became inconvenient when
the invention of gunpowder made battle more a matter of
skill and luck than strength and courage. Marko Kraljevic
saw this when in a Bulgarian lay he lamented that the invention of the rifle meant the demolition of heroes such as he.[8]
Milton too saw this when in the War of Heaven he sends up
conventional epic warfare and modern warfare with the forces
of Satan discovering gunpowder from the bowels of the earth;
the crude anatomical imagery gives the game away.[9]

In the nineteenth century the rise of nationalism and the
Romantic admiration for nature's children untrammelled by
the pressures of civilisation gave an unexpected lease of
life to the hero in unexpected places. It is hard to understand the admiration for Ossian, the world's most bogus epic
poet. Byron's claim that *Don Juan* is an epic poem which he
makes with his tongue clearly in his cheek by saying that he
has twelve books, stories at sea and all the technical appa-
ratus of epic becomes a little less bogus in the episode
with Haidée, a true child of nature. Byron like Don Juan and
Childe Harold found a kind of heroic fulfilment in the Balkans, and almost simultaneously some kind of epic heroism
was found in the deeds of the Greek klephts and Balkan
haiduchs fighting anachronistically rifles with swords, in
the same fashion as a hundred and fifty years later other
heroes fought Stukas with rifles, both kinds of battle being
celebrated with the same kind of poem as had been composed
for Kosovo.

But heroes do not make an epic poem, and the great epic
poems succeed in spite rather than because of their heroes.
Achilles is undoubtedly heroic; the idea that he is a tragic
hero like Oedipus or Othello whose tragic flaw leads him to

disaster and disgrace is an alien importation from another
genre, since in spite of modern squeamishness we must recognise that it is in the moments of his alleged debasement,
namely his laments for Patroclus and his cruel treatment of
Hector, that Achilles is at his most magnificent. In any
case Achilles is not there for much of the *Iliad*. In the
Odyssey Odysseus too is not always present, and his heroism
is marred by rashness or tempered by discretion. Aeneas is
an improbable hero, although we need not go as far as Vol-
taire in despising him and his fellow heroes for being so
insipid, or as far as Dryden who faced by Aeneas's embarras-
sing lapses from grace covered up for him by mistranslating
the *Aeneid*.[10] Dante especially goes out of his way to say
that he is no hero, and the various candidates for the hero
of *Paradise Lost*, Satan, God, Christ, Gabriel, Adam and Milton himself prove that the equation of an epic poem with a
poem about a hero does not work.

After these unsuccessful attempts to define an epic in too
narrow terms we are driven back on more vague but more successful general definitions. An epic is not simple, but it
is single. The wholeness of the epic vision may be one
reason why Aeschylus said, if he did say it, that his plays
were slices from the banquets of Homer. In spite of Professor Gould's modesty in claiming that he does not understand
this remark he does in his essay show ways in which Aeschylus is both similar to and different from Homer, and he also
shows that the differences are differences of scale. A tragedy even if magnified into a trilogy like the *Oresteia* cannot encompass a whole world, as an epic can and must.

Two devices that the epic uses to make itself more of a
whole are the flashback to the past and the prophecy of the
future. Time is difficult in drama, and no wonder Aristotle
and neo-classical critics fussed nervously about the Unities.
But it is not difficult for epic writers to cast the reader
forward to the future and drive him backwards towards the
past. The fall of Troy, the descent into the underworld,
Aeneas's shield, the war in Heaven and the visions Michael
shows Adam are obvious examples. Dante teases the reader
with his juggling of past, present and future, as he writes
some years after 1300 about figures who have died before
1300 talking to him in that year. The *Odyssey* contains both
a flashback and a prophecy, ineptly copied, like the conclaves of gods and catalogues of ships, by inferior epic
writers, but used by Virgil and Milton to make their epic
timeless; in the *Odyssey* the adventures of Odysseus and his
visit to the shades may seem to operate on a more super-
ficial level, as adding the spice of adventure, although
they do show Odysseus maturing and being able to learn from

his mistakes. The *Iliad* too, though apparently firmly set in
a short period during the tenth year of the Trojan war,
looks both forward and back. In the third book Helen's
appearance on the walls of Troy pointing out Agamemnon,
Odysseus and Ajax to Priam is a reminder of the first year
of the war, and in the last six books Achilles several times
gives and is given grim intimations of his own mortality.

Mr Merchant reminds us of how Greece with its three thousand years of epic tradition finds it easier to link past,
present and future, but Professor Gould reminds us that
there are times unsuitable for epic. The present age would
seem in the same way as the fifth century B.C. to be a
period when such rapid changes are taking place that there
is no place for the reflective epic vision. Both periods are
ones in which drama has flourished. The Renaissance, another
period of rapid change, saw both drama and epic, and this
might seem to disprove the theory that the epic needs a particular 'Zeitgeist', although we could argue that as the
particular feature of the Renaissance was the discovery of
the classical past it falls into a rather different category
from other periods of rapid intellectual change. Alternatively it could be argued that the Renaissance epics of Boiardo,
Ariosto, Tasso, Spenser and Camoës do not quite succeed because they are unable to adapt to a universe in which the
new philosophy put all in doubt; their treatment of the miraculous is an acknowledged weakness.

It may be coincidental that Virgil, Dante and Milton wrote
their epics after a gruelling civil war, in which their emotions had been heavily involved. The reverberations of these
wars certainly cast heavy shadows over the epics of all
three writers. Homer cannot be fitted into this pattern,
unless we count the Dark Ages as such a war, although we
know so little about Homer that we might as well try and
make the Trojan war the appropriate civil war. Shakespeare
who did not write epics, also lived in a period when civil
strife was a constant threat, and this certainly cast a shadow over his work; if it is possible to fit Shakespeare into
any philosophical mould there is a cosmic toryism in his
historical plays and tragedies which begins to approach the
certainty of the epic vision.

For if the epic has anything to commend it, it has
authority. Mr Merchant has used this word to describe the
achievements of modern Greek poets. Authority is now an un-
fashionable term, suggesting old fashioned imperialistic
elitist vices that were once considered virtues, but are despised now in an age of committees and compromises. Such was
not the case at any rate on the surface in Victorian times,
when it might seem that epic would have flourished. And

indeed there are epic traits in the Victorian kaleidoscope.
Tennyson's poem on Virgil rings a note that wielders of less
stately measures have found it hard to echo. His *Idylls of
the King* reminds us superficially of the epic, although all
but the most ignorant reader cannot help feeling sadly, as
Tennyson must have felt, the difference between the muddied
muddled battle in the Western mist between Arthur and Mor-
dred, which nobody wins, and the clear hard vision of Homer,
where might triumphs, and the sweet sad insight of Virgil,
where right is eventually victorious. Browning's *The Ring
and the Book* has authority but lacks wholeness; it is a collection of dramatic pieces which only our present contempt
for the Victorian age, and the Victorian age's contempt for
the drama has prevented from being properly appreciated.
Matthew Arnold's attempt at an epic fragment in *Sohrab and
Rustum* is heavily derivative, but shows as well as *Dover
Beach* the modern uncertainty lurking behind the mask of Victorian confidence. William Morris, though wavering between
Norse and Classical models, and at times coming dangerously
close to pastiche is less sensitive than Tennyson, Browning
and Arnold, but more original; students of the epic could do
worse than study *Sigurd the Volsung*.

In one of the few relatively modern attempts to come to
grips with a definition of epic Northrop Frye shows both the
dangers and the attractions of a schematic division of literature by genres. In *The Anatomy of Criticism*[11] Frye makes
Homer, Virgil and Milton's epics encyclopaedic works in the
high mimetic mode, the *Iliad* being an epic of wrath, the
Odyssey an epic of return, the *Aeneid* an epic of wrath and
return, while *Paradise Lost* puts all three classical works
into 'a wider archetypal context'; Dante's *Divine Comedy* is
regarded together with the *Faerie Queen* as an encyclopaedic
work in the romantic mode, and an analogical epic. The poly-
syllabic definitions may discourage the student from realis-
ing that Frye is only putting into slightly more elaborate
words his own feeling that Dante is in a different category
from other epics. The lumping together of the well known
epics as encyclopaedic works together with such other master-
pieces as Proust's *A la Recherche du Temps Perdu* and Joyce's
Ulysses encourages those who look to wholeness as a criterion for the epic, but is clearly discouraging to those who
look for something a little narrower. In the twentieth century encyclopaedias though useful are hardly regarded as
authoritative in academic circles; they become rapidly dated
in the same way as even Northrop Frye seems curiously old-
fashioned. The epic seems to many as antique as the dinosaur,
but it cannot but be useful for all students of literature
to consider aspects of the epic.

NOTES

1. J. Hagin, *The Epic Hero and the Decline of Heroic Poetry*
   (Bern, 1964) provides some useful information about
   Blackmore's epic poetry and J. Wight Duff, *A Literary
   History of Rome in the Silver Age* (London, 1964) puts
   Silius Italicus in his place.
2. S. Koljevic, *The Epic in the Making* (Oxford, 1980).
3. Horace, *Satires*, 2.1. 12-15. Pope parodies Blackmore in
   his imitation of this satire.
4. I am grateful to Professor C.J. Rawson for drawing my
   attention to Pope's remarks which may be found in the
   Twickenham edition of Pope's *Poems*, (London, 1967) vol.7,
   p.13, vol.10, p.390. The *Dunciad* citation of Milton is
   in the note to 2.63 referring to *Paradise Lost*, 2.947.
5. D. Wilson, *The Life and Times of Vuk Stefanovic
   Karadzic* (Oxford, 1970).
6. D. Comparetti, *The Traditional Poetry of the Finns*,
   trans. I.M. Anderson (London, 1898).
7. *Inferno*, 1.108-9. *Paradiso*, 17.46-8. On the other hand
   Dante, not unnaturally prejudiced against the Florence
   of his own times, makes Caccaguida speak nostalgically
   of Florence when it was a small city-state.
8. C. Manning and R. Smol-Stocki, *The History of Modern
   Bulgarian Literature*, (Westport, 1960) pp.169-70.
9. *Paradise Lost*, 6.568-94.
10. *Candide* ed. R. Pomeau (Paris, 1959), p.198. For Dryden's
    faults as a translator L. Proudfoot, *Dryden's Aeneid and
    its Seventeenth Century Predecessors* (Manchester, 1960).
11. *Anatomy of Criticism* (New York, 1957).

Index